TOTAL SUCCESS!

By **T.J. Rohleder**
(a.k.a "The Blue Jeans Millionaire")

BE SURE TO CHECK OUT OTHER GREAT TITLES FROM THE BLUE JEANS MILLIONAIRE LIBRARY:

The Magic Pill
The 2-Step Marketing Secret Than Never Fails!
The Wow Factor!
3 Steps to Instant Profits!
Instant Cash Flow!
Money Machine
The Power of Hype!
Stealth Marketing
Jump... And the Net Will Appear!
Think Bigger

TABLE OF CONTENTS

Introduction:

By T.J. Rohleder

TOTAL SUCCESS IS YOURS!!!

Congratulations on your decision to read this book. After all, most people wish they had more money, but how many are willing to pick up and study a book that can help them do it? Very few.

Yes, most people want ALL of the greatest benefits that life and business has to offer — but they don't want to pay the price to get these things. And they are certainly afraid to take the kinds of RISKS that they must take to get what they want.

Plus, most people give up way too soon. The very first time they experience any major setbacks or adversity, they pack-it-up and are on to the next thing.

And yet, when you study the lives of the richest and most powerful entrepreneurs who started with little or even nothing and turned it into massive sums of money, you'll see that they had or developed the ability to RISE ABOVE all of the pain, problems, and adversities that stop most people from achieving the success they want. This key factor [of 'going from failure to failure without losing your enthusiasm' and refusing to quit — no matter what] more than anything else, is the greatest secret for their TOTAL SUCCESS.

TOTAL SUCCESS!

It will be the key secret for all of the success and money that you want and need, too.

So please go over Chapter One to learn more about this secret of total success. Then use this powerful idea [which came from a quote by the great leader, Winston Churchill] in conjunction with all of the other powerful methods and strategies in the remainder chapters to make all the money you want, need, and truly deserve.

And Remember This...

All the money you want and need to achieve your biggest goals and dreams is out there waiting for you! Yes, it's out there — RIGHT NOW — as you're reading my words. Where is it? That's simple: it's in the wallets, purses, and available lines of credit of millions of people who are searching for the benefits that YOU can provide to them in the form of various products and services you offer.

It sounds so simple — BECAUSE IT IS!!! Of course, it's NOT easy. And yet, the more you want something, the easier it is to get it. In fact, if you want it BAD ENOUGH, you'll push yourself harder than you've ever pushed yourself, but IT WON'T SEEM LIKE WORK AT ALL...

So now that you know where the money is [re-read the above paragraph] — the only question is: 'HOW DO YOU GET IT?' Well, it turns out that the answer to that question is rather simple, too. I'll give it to you in four words:

Become a Marketing Expert

Marketing is the process you go through to attract and retain the very best customers who want what you sell. Just get enough people to consistently give you enough money... often enough... for a large enough profit margin per transaction and all the money you want will be yours. Yes, it's that simple! And when you COMBINE that idea with the secrets you'll get in the first chapter of this book, you can make all the money you've ever dreamed of making!

So please keep those simple ideas in mind as you go through this book. Have fun reading each Chapter and THINK DEEPLY about how you can use all of the powerful ideas and strategies I'm about to share with you...

Here's What You'll Discover In This Book

This book gives you some of the most powerful business and marketing secrets I've used to generate millions of dollars in my own business. The first chapter is also the title of this book. It tells you how to take VERY BIG, but very calculated risks. As you'll discover; you can use the secrets behind Winston Churchill's great quote as the FOUNDATION of your TOTAL SUCCESS! Just go through chapter one and get some of our greatest secrets for doing this. Then use the ideas and methods to begin achieving your biggest goals and dreams! Then take the tip, tricks, and strategies I'll give you in the first chapter and use them in conjunction with all of the other great marketing secrets you'll get in the other eleven chapters in this book. Do this and you can be on your way to making all the money you've ever dreamed of making!

And to reward you for purchasing this book, I have...

A great FREE business-building gift for you!

Yes, I have a gift waiting for you that can DRAMATICALLY INCREASE YOUR SALES AND PROFITS! Here's what it's all about: I spent TEN FULL YEARS writing down all of the greatest marketing and success secrets I discovered during that time period. Each day, I took a few notes and, at the end of a decade, I had a GIANT LIST of 6,159 powerful secrets! This list is ALMOST 1,000 PAGES of hardcore money-making ideas and strategies!** **Best of all, this massive collection is now YOURS ABSOLUTELY FREE!** Just go to: www.6159FreeSecrets.com and get it NOW! As you'll see, this complete collection of 6,159 of my greatest marketing and success secrets, far more valuable than those you can buy from others for $495 to $997, is absolutely **FREE.** No cost, no obligation.

Why am I giving away this GIANT COLLECTION of secrets that took ONE DECADE to discover and compile— FOR FREE? That's simple: I believe many of the people who receive these 6,159 secrets in this huge 955 page PDF document will want to obtain some of our other books and audio programs and participate in our special COACHING PROGRAMS. However, you are NOT obligated to buy anything—now or ever.

I know you're serious about making more money or you wouldn't be reading this. So go to: www.6159FreeSecrets.com

and get this complete collection of 6,159 of my greatest marketing and success secrets right now! **You'll get this GREAT FREE GIFT in the next few minutes, just for letting me add you to my Client mailing list,** and I'll stay in CLOSE TOUCH with you... and do all I can to help you make even more money with my proven marketing strategies and methods.

So with all this said, let's begin...

** WARNING: This complete collection of 6,159 marketing and success secrets contains MANY CONTROVERSIAL ideas and methods. Also, it was originally written for MY EYES ONLY and for a few VERY CLOSE FRIENDS. Therefore, the language is X-RATED in some places [I got VERY EXCITED when I wrote many of these ideas and used VERY FOUL LANGUAGE to get my ideas across!] so 'IF' you are EASILY OFFENDED or do NOT want to read anything OFFENSIVE, then please do both of us a favor and DO NOT go to my website and download this FREE gift. THANK YOU for your understanding.

CHAPTER ONE

Success is the ability
to outrun failure!

Success is the Ability to Outrun Failure!

While the title is meant to be a bit tongue-in-cheek, it's appropriate—and it really sticks in your brain.

Winston Churchill once said, **"Success is the ability to go from failure to failure without losing your enthusiasm."** I think that strikes right to the heart of the matter, because the only true failure occurs when you give up. It took Thomas Edison about a thousand tries to invent the light bulb. What if he'd given up after failure #100, or #312 for that matter? I doubt we'd be in the dark right now, but we probably wouldn't celebrate Edison's inventiveness, either. The day you finally give up on your dream is the day you fail, not before—not even if you've been fruitlessly working at being successful for decades. Let me repeat: **Until you give up on your dream, you're not a failure.**

Now, yes, a particular enterprise may go under because it can't pay its bills, or a certain promotion may not go the way you planned. Technically, those can be considered failures; but in the broader scheme of things, they're just setbacks on your road to success. Disappointments, frustrations, heartache, and pain are all parts of business. You'll inevitably experience highs and lows; and that's one of the reasons why people both love business and hate it at the same time. **Business isn't an either/or kind of thing; it's like a roller coaster ride, both**

thrilling and scary at the same time. You have to be willing to take on the good and the bad alike.

So many people do fail in business, though—because they give up. They quit. They say enough is enough. I've been fully self-employed since December 1985, and since that time I've spoken with hundreds of people who have told me, "Oh, I tried business, and it didn't work for me." They're everywhere. Most of them are bitter and cynical about it... or they're still heartbroken about the fact that they gave up.

I love business, but I know very well how difficult it can be. **You have to constantly forge ahead with your eyes wide open, recognizing all the market forces that are working to destroy you, to wipe out your profits, to put you out of business.** There's increased competition everywhere—and the customer has more choices than ever before, which puts you at a significant disadvantage. With this power to choose, the customer is no longer merely king; they're more like a spoiled child dictator, because they know they can make just about any demand and have their whims attended to. This forces us marketers to be sharper than ever if we want to survive.

I'm not telling you this to discourage you. Consider it an espresso shot of reality, an attempt not just to open your eyes to the difficulties of the marketplace, but also to jazz you up as you survey those challenges. **You have to be super-sharp to compete successfully, because the harsh reality is that it *is* tough out there.** It's damned tough—and if you expect to make a lot of money, you've got to be tough yourself. You've got to realize that there will be plenty of times along the way when things just don't work out the way you want them to. When that happens, you have to pick yourself back up, dust yourself off, and keep moving forward. **You can't let *anything* stop you for long.** That's part of what this "outrunning failure" concept is all about: continuing to move, motivating yourself. Fear is a great motivator, and so is the truth. What I've just given you is a small sample of the truth.

You also have to realize that the markets are constantly changing. They're evolving. They're *re*volving. **What works in one quarter may not work the next, so another way you have to strive to outrun failure is by constantly testing new things, and never resting on your laurels for too long.** Pace yourself, but push yourself. Don't burn yourself out, but don't idle along either. You've got to work very, very hard on yourself and your business, and you've got to decide once and for all that nothing is going to stop you. You just can't let it happen—and there *will* be all kinds of things that will disappoint you, frustrate you, and infuriate you along the way.

Heartbreak and pain are inevitable in business, just as they are in the rest of your life. Never pretend otherwise.

And again, I'm not saying that to discourage you. That's the last thing I want to do, because business is a wonderful thing. **I can honestly say that it includes some of the best things that life has to offer, along with all these negative things.** It's just life on steroids, you see. Yes, there will be problems, setbacks, disappointments, frustrations, and heartache to go along with the triumph and joy. There will be stressful times; there will be tough times. And it's during those times that you run into the "make or break" situations. **If you can push through the bad patches, you end up stronger and wiser.** You recommit yourself. You become better. You find places within yourself that you didn't know existed. You see things you don't see when everything is going smoothly. Ultimately, those bad times can actually be good for you—*if* you refuse to give up.

Everybody wants life to be easy; that's part of being human. **But ironically, the best way to make things easier is by forcing yourself to become stronger—and to do that you have to keep pushing, constantly, no matter what.** I wish I had figured that out earlier in my career; but the truth is, even just a few years ago, I couldn't have expressed it so clearly. The way to make yourself stronger is to push yourself, especially when you have to push yourself through those hard times.

About six years ago, I came very close to losing it all. I was so deeply in debt that I was what I call a reverse millionaire: I owed more than a million dollars more than my net worth. In a way, I was worth more money dead than alive, given the size of my life insurance policy... but even that wasn't really true, because if I'd died, my heirs would have had to repay all that debt out of the insurance settlement.

The point is, I was in serious trouble. I'd over-leveraged myself on some promotions that just fell apart on us. I pointed out earlier that what works during one quarter of the year may not work in the next. Well, I know that from personal experience. We were flying high for a while, just rolling in the dough. Frankly, we were making more money in some months than we used to make in entire years. **But the higher you fly, the harder you can crash; and I did crash.** Suddenly, I was in deep trouble indeed—and I didn't know what to do.

Instead of declaring bankruptcy, I decided to stick it out. I've got a great staff here at M.O.R.E.; **I've surrounded myself with lots of people who are much smarter than I am. With their support and guidance, we pulled the company out of that pit of debt and climbed back up the mountain... though the way was very painful at times.** Now I'm overjoyed that I didn't declare bankruptcy, despite the terrible situation and the long, slow haul up out of that deep hole. I won't lie: the climb out was very difficult emotionally, mentally, spiritually, and even physically. It wasn't a bed of roses for the people who work closely with me, either. Some of the things I put them through were severe. And yes, some of the problems I put my creditors through were terrible.

It was a bad time all around, as bad as it's ever been. I've never gone through such a difficult period before.

We had to let a lot of our people go at one point. I did a mass firing—I just pulled a bunch of employees into in one big room, and laid them off all at once. It was a horrible experience, and let's just say that it didn't go quite as smoothly as I had envisioned it beforehand. **Unsurprisingly, they were angry at me, and there was some yelling and screaming and it wasn't very pretty.** Some of those people I was happy to get rid of; most of them I wasn't. It was what I envision as hell on earth... but I did it. I did what I had to do to survive.

Ultimately, that experience, as bad as it was, made me stronger. **I got through it, and I'm glad I didn't give up.** There's real strength in going through difficult periods, in learning the harsh lessons you have to learn, in being forced to develop new knowledge and skills and abilities, and leaning

17

even harder on the people you surround yourself with.

I can't emphasize enough that you've got to surround yourself with the right people. **That team you build to achieve your goals and dreams is instrumental to your success.** That's where the real strength in business comes from anyway: the synergistic efforts of a group of people working well together. When times get tough, you'll find yourself relying on them more and more—just as they rely on you.

And here's another point I want you to remember: nothing is ever a complete failure if you can reach into the ruins and find one brick you can build on. While I'm not going to tell you that failure is necessarily a good thing, it doesn't have to be devastating if you're willing to learn from it. Look at it this way: **in almost every case, true success is built upon many previous outcomes—and some of those outcomes will inevitably be failures.** By failing 1,000 times to successfully create a light bulb, Thomas Edison learned what didn't work. As every scientist knows, negative outcomes are important, too.

Too many people get hung up on individual failures, just as they get hung up on individual successes… and both can be detrimental to your business. You shouldn't look at things that way. The outcomes you achieve in your business, whether successes or failures, just determine the next step you need take, not the sum total of your success or failure as a businessperson. **Business is a journey. It's a story that you're writing into existence, and it doesn't end until you decide it does, when you put that pen down and close the book for good.**

So don't obsess about things that don't work out. **When**

you're on a long journey, you need to make course adjustments occasionally. That's what an airplane does, after all; the pilot is constantly making minor corrections on the way to the final destination. Just because the plane goes a certain distance in a slightly wrong direction doesn't mean that the flight won't end up where it's supposed to; the crew just nudges it back on course. If you're flying from Chicago to Hong Kong, as Chris Lakey has in the past, the pilot doesn't just get the plane to cruising altitude and then turn on the autopilot for 15 hours until they finally arrive magically at Hong Kong. Various factors will put the plane slightly off course during the flight, so the pilot needs to check that course periodically and make the necessary adjustments to get it back in the groove.

In the case of the Chicago-to-Hong Kong flight Chris was on, they flew up and over the North Pole to get there, and you could watch it all on video. They had a GPS route up on a TV screen right in front of Chris's seat, and he could clearly see little jags in the course. Those were the pilot's adjustments. **Now, even if you were to look at each one of those jags as a failure, that wouldn't mean the flight as a whole was a failure.** Obviously they got there. **Those little jags were just adjustments on the way to the final destination, that's all.**

That happens with your success journey, too. **The things you encounter along the way are just parts of the whole story.** So if you were to look back on your life as you wrote your autobiography, sure, you'd see both ends; but you would also see all the course adjustments along the way. Some of them you might classify as failures; some you might classify as successes. Whatever the case may be, they aren't the story in

TOTAL SUCCESS!

whole; they're only parts of it. **How you adjust to those parts—how you integrate the successes and outrun the failures—will determine your next moves.**

Chris likes to play a game on his smartphone called "Words With Friends"; it's like Scrabble for your phone. You play, they play, and you're trying to use the letters you're dealt to build words and score points. Sometimes Chris makes a bad move. Does that mean the game's over? No! It means that, hopefully, it doesn't cost him too many points; and next time he gets a turn, he can adjust and build off that mistake and make a better score. Ultimately, his ability to recover from a bad move in Words With Friends determines his ability to win the overall game. **As with business, outrunning the failure and deciding your next move is more important than the move that got you into the muck in the first place.**

The worst thing you can do is get stuck in the mud and let failure catch up to you; because if failure is consistently all about you, then suddenly you'll be about failure, and that will be the death of your business. Your ability to outrun failure—to make your next move, and move on from there—will determine your ultimate success. Just move on. Nobody can change the past—so you might as well just learn from it and look forward to the future.

Keep falling back in love with what got you excited about the business to begin with. Surround yourself with the very best people. **Think harder and deeper than you've thought before.** The solutions are out there. Know that when you get into a bad spot and you feel like there's no hope, *those feelings are lying to you*. You always have options.

One last thing: **you can benefit greatly by studying the biographies of people who have already made it.** If you're not an avid reader, that's fine. There are plenty of documentary films that you can rent or buy, so there's no excuse for you *not* to study other people's lives. If you do it enough, you'll see all kinds of push and pull, hard times and people overcoming hard times, lots of drama. You'll see the times when they suffered setback after setback. You'll learn about all the adversities, the headaches, the hassles, the challenges, the disappointments, the nightmares that they had to live through, the times when they didn't think they would make it, when everything and everyone seemed to be turning against them.

And yet, part of what made them successful—the reason you can read books or watch documentaries about them now—is that they persevered. **They went through all that muck and mire, and they didn't give up.** They kept believing in themselves, believing in the people who surrounded them, believing in their original visions, and they kept fighting. **The more they fought, the more they developed the skills and circumstances they needed to pull them out of their slumps.** Almost no one gets from Point A to Point B in a straight line; there are inevitable course adjustments along the way... just like in Chris's 15-hour flight from Chicago to Hong Kong.

Remember one of the basic laws of physics: **an object in motion tends to stay in motion. So keep moving. Keep outrunning failure.**

CHAPTER TWO

**Everybody loves
an offer they perceive
is just for them.**

**The things they want
the most are the things
others cannot get!**

Everyone Loves an Exclusive Offer!

Exclusive offers are very attractive to the average consumer. In fact, **the more a prospect perceives that your offer has been designed with them** *specifically* **in mind, the more they're going to want it.** Which leads us to a corollary: the things that people want the most are the things that other people can't get. In other words, the more they feel that an offer's intended for just anybody, the less they're likely to want it.

Therefore, **you always have to build something unique into whatever you're selling, in order to draw people in.** The hard part here is that there's nothing that's particularly unique anymore... and there hasn't been, really, for thousands of years. As the Bible puts it, "There's nothing new under the sun." That's part of the Old Testament, so someone pointed that out well before the arrival of Christ himself. Despite this fact—or, perhaps, because of it—**everybody in every marketplace** *wants* **something new and special.** So if you want to make money with your offers, you have to make your best effort to create such things, so you can differentiate what you're offering from all the similar offers out there.

Here at M.O.R.E., Inc., **the best examples of what I would call exclusive offers—products that fit like a hand to a glove, so that when people get one they say, "This was designed for me"—are our websites.** We've sold millions of dollars worth of "beta tester" promotions since we started developing websites back in the mid-1990s, when the Internet was first taking off. Back then, people might pay $20,000-30,000 for something you can get now for less than $1,000—and often for less than $500. Well, we were one of the very first development companies to offer inexpensive websites to the average consumer. We've specialized in what we call "beta tester" offers, which is where we release a group of websites to testers because they're not quite ready for the marketplace yet—there's always something new that has to be checked out. But we don't release them for free; **we simply give our customers a very special deal on a block of websites.** They're happy because they got them for a low price, and we're happy because we made some money *and* got the bugs worked out of our websites during the testing process.

For example: for many years, we sold different versions of a block of 300 websites to our customers. We were always revising them, making them better, trying new features, and the like. **We'd give our customers 50 of those websites for a phenomenally low price, making it clear that they were getting this deal because these were beta versions that hadn't been tested fully.** We'd tell them we needed beta testers to help us get the bugs out of them—and then we would deliver the sites to them and just blow them away! They would be shocked when they saw what we'd given them; **the quality was high, and the price was a bargain.** Oftentimes we'd throw in a few years of free hosting, too—and all for as little as $9 for all 50 sites, though the price was more likely to be $29 or $39.

No sooner did they get those sites than we'd follow-up

with a special offer, just for them, for an additional block of 250 websites that were similar to the 50 they'd purchased. Our offer pointed out, "Look, you're already a beta tester for our first 50 websites…", and we thanked them profusely. They had a chance to go on the Internet and look over their sites, so we demonstrated to them that we were trustworthy. In all these ways, we proved that our offer was everything that we said it was. They were already sold on the concept of being beta testers for these first 50 websites, so we knew that this custom-tailored offer for an additional 250 websites was the perfect upsell.

This was a true "hand in glove" offer. Now, think about that; because that's how it has to work. Visualize a glove that your hand fits into perfectly. It's wintertime as I'm writing this, and it's very, very cold here in Goessel, Kansas. Most of us who live here don't mind the cold weather… as long as we're dressed for it. So we all wear gloves whenever we go outside. Think about how a nice, well-fitting glove feels, and how warm it keeps your hands. Think of how warm a prospect feels when they fit perfectly into an offer—when it feels like it's been tailored especially for them.

Our beta tester offer was custom-designed just for our existing customers, and it gave them more of what they'd already bought from us. We knew that they were already sold, and it let us speak to that group in a way that let them *know* that the offer was just for them. We've done that with other types of offers, where we try to give our prospects a small piece of the much bigger piece that we want to sell them later. With our websites, that's easy to do.

In the next few months, we're going to be developing a

new offer where we give our beta testers 100 websites to start with, and then we're going to follow up with an offer for an additional 1,000—or maybe even more. We might even start out by giving them 240 websites, and then offer them 2,400 more. **Those kinds of deals just blow people away, because those deals speak directly to what the customers want.** It gives them more of what they already had, and it's exclusive for them.

And remember, the second part of this strategy is that the things people want the most are the things that others can't get. As I write this, we're putting together copy for a new seminar that's coming up in the next month. Over this past weekend, I decided to limit the seminar to just 73 people, each of whom can bring a guest of their choice. Now, why did I do that? Because it made the product super-exclusive. They know that if they're the 74th person to try to sign up, they're not going to get in. It's special—and that's what people really want.

You know, in some ways people are very, very complex; and the smarter they are, the more complicated they are. But in other ways (especially from an emotional standpoint), people are very simple. **Once of the simplicities within the complexity of human behavior is the fact that we all want what other people can't have.** We all want things that are special, created just for us. We all want to feel important; in fact, many of us are *desperate* to feel important. These days, most people don't; they just feel like numbers, or walking wallets. The more you can do to show them how much you appreciate them, that you want to give them access to something very limited, something that other people can't get—the better they'll respond.

We've got another extremely limited offer going at the

moment that has a very firm cut-off point. If a prospect misses out on it, then someone else is going to take their position; we're very clear that there are only so many of these positions available. **In a situation like this one, people fight to get in, so they can lock themselves in and not have to worry about somebody else coming along and grabbing that exclusive offer.** That being the case, the profit potential for an offer like this is immense.

These things don't just happen by accident: you have to work to make them special. So how do you accomplish this? By becoming intimately aware of every aspect of the marketplace. As I've emphasized repeatedly in this book, **you must put yourself in the shoes of the people you're trying to reach, and learn every detail you can about them.** What's most important to them? What conversations are going on in their heads, right this moment? How can you strongly communicate your offer in such a way as to make it more desirable?

I just got an email from a man I spent some time with last summer, during our Branson Seminar in Branson, Missouri. He and I had talked about an idea for making millions of dollars back then, and now, months later, he's emailing me with some information on this offer. I've read his email five times—and I still don't understand what the hell he's talking about. He rambled on for three pages and didn't tell me a single thing. He didn't make the offer attractive or exclusive one bit. If it weren't for the fact that I really care about this man, I wouldn't have paid any attention to the offer at all—I would have scrapped it in a second. But instead I'm trying to work with him, trying to go back and forth with him to understand what he's trying to say.

TOTAL SUCCESS!

Your offers can't be like that. They have to be crystal clear, so your prospects can instantly see the advantages you've set up for them. **They've got to immediately grasp just how perfect your offer is for them—to perceive, just from looking, that it will fit them like a glove.** To achieve this kind of transparency, you must develop and maintain an intimate awareness of the people you're trying to reach. Learn what's most important to them, and how you can clearly (and I do mean *clearly*) communicate the most important benefits in the shortest period of time, so that they'll instantly see your offer for what it is and will instantly be attracted to it.

It really is amazing how human psychology dominates this equation—how much it feeds into developing effective sales tactics. **You're fighting the tide if you fail to take into account the psychological aspects of business;** the cold math isn't all you need to help you sell your products and opportunities. The exclusivity factor really weighs heavily here, and you can see this when you look at real life examples of how people go about their daily lives and exercise their spending habits. Consider how people respond to any Limited Edition of just about anything. **If they know that only a certain number of a product was made, then all of a sudden the value goes up.** Think of an art print that an artist created only a few hundred copies of; that alone can cause the value to soar. Now, suppose he signed and numbered a select handful of those items. If you have one of those, then your piece of art is even more valuable—simply because there are very few of them available. This kind of exclusivity is what makes most unique art pieces worth more than generic, copied pieces.

When Chris Lakey was a kid, he used to collect baseball and basketball cards. You know, it's one thing just to open a pack of cards, and know that the cards inside are also owned by kids all over the U.S., and that a particular card you're holding is worth a few pennies because it's the same as millions of other cards out there. But usually, some of the cards are available only in limited editions—and you might get lucky. The card company will print on the card pack the odds of what you might pull out of a particular pack of cards. It might be that one out of every 100,000 packs contains an autographed card by whoever happens to be the hottest person in the sport. Chris remembers specifically that back in the early 1990s, Shaquille O'Neal was the hot basketball rookie—and so it was a real thrill to pull a Limited Edition Shaquille O'Neal card. Kids would open dozens of packs of cards trying to get one.

Well, why would you care about any Limited Edition card? **Because it's exclusive.** If you have one, it's likely that no one else you know has one. Chris remembers pulling one of the Limited Edition Shaquille O'Neal cards from a pack once, when he was 15 or 16 years old —and although it wasn't signed, it was worth about $120 at the time. It was just a piece of heavy paper with a picture of a basketball player on it, but the fact that there were only so many of them to go around and *he had one* made him value it more than any old sports card.

His 13-year-old son still has that card stashed somewhere in his room, sealed in a big, heavy piece of protective hard plastic. It's worth ten bucks or so now. But Chris is hoping that one day, that card will become worth something again, and maybe his son can sell it for a little bit of money at some point...

or just keep it for the novelty's sake. The point here is that back when it was new, Chris really wanted that card; he wanted all the cards like that. He spent a lot of time and money acquiring meaningless packs of cards to try to find that one Limited Edition card that he knew he wanted the most—**because if he got it, then other people didn't have it. That's the way people are with all kinds of things.**

Similarly, some people like to drive Limited Edition sports cars. If it happens that the manufacturer made only 1,000 of that particular auto, then they're willing to spend more to acquire one. You probably have examples in your own life where you're like that for one thing or another. In our areas of interest or need, we love to get exclusive offers—offers that we perceive are available only to us, or at least to only a few people. **We look for deals that aren't available just anywhere.** We rummage through garage sales looking for that perfect find... that one thing you jump on because no one else can get it, and here it is right in front of you! Let's say you go to the Salvation Army Thrift Store, and you find something they somehow mispriced—something that should have been sold for more. Suddenly, you've scored a good deal on something that isn't available to anybody else—and that makes you feel really good, doesn't it?

That's how your prospects feel when you present them with a perfect fit that you offer for a compelling price. **And it doesn't necessarily have to be a specific item; it could be something more general that lets them know how much you appreciate doing business with them.** Recently, Chris tells me, he received an email from a big electronics chain that said they were having a special after-hours event, and he was invited. Apparently the ad wasn't compelling enough to get him out of his home to drive that half-hour to where the store was located, because he didn't go; but the point is, they *did* extend the invitation to this exclusive event for their "preferred customers." They wanted him to feel special. Now, no doubt they were thronged with people who brought in that little slip from the email that was their ticket to attend the after-hours event... so they could spend money with the store that had made them feel special. In a sense, they all had Golden Tickets that let them get better deals on some items they wanted anyway; and having been made to feel special, do you suppose those people will return and spend more money? Of course they will.

We all want to feel special like that; **so as a marketer, you need to find a way to give your customers and prospects that feeling, so they can appreciate being on the inside.** Nobody wants something that's readily available. Have you ever seen someone wearing a ring with a stone made of coal or sand? Probably not. Nobody wants a sand ring; they want a diamond ring. Why? Because diamonds are rare, and therefore in demand. The cost is high, and a diamond ring is much more exclusive than any plain ring; so people want one. And they don't want just any diamond either, or they would be more likely to accept the inexpensive synthetic ones. No, people want the best natural diamonds possible, diamonds of a high grade, especially those that are naturally colored; those are especially scarce. In other words, people prefer the stones that are genuinely rare, of extraordinarily limited availability.

Exclusive things make people feel good, which is why you have to carefully evaluate precisely what your customers really,

really want the most—and then give it a twist that makes it even more special. What do they feel would be an exclusive buy for them? What do they feel would put them on the inside, put them in the know, or to put them in a position where they can get something that no one else can get? Maybe that's a limited time offer, available to a small group of people, like the one I mentioned earlier. Maybe you find another way to pull out the stops for a preferred group of customers. The point is, you've *got* to come up with that angle that everybody wants, but only a handful can get. People will pay big money for exclusivity; so when you add it to your offers, you'll see your sales will increase.

And one of the things you can do when you're positioning yourself like this is to use what information you have to your advantage. Let's say you know that 10% of your customers are likely to take advantage of your offer, and you have 100 customers (just to have a round number to simplify the math). Well, why not tighten up that offer and make it exclusive to only the first 10 people who respond? Just come right out and say it in your sales copy—and be sure to stick to that number like glue, so you have credibility on your side the next time you do it. **I guarantee that people will respond to that promise of exclusivity.** Set the number wherever you're comfortable. You might even bump it up to 12 or 15, but cut it off when you get there; otherwise, what is your exclusivity worth? **If you're worried about the fact that making something exclusive will limit your profits, then juice up the value some and raise the price.**

And in any case, you'll probably have a lot more than 100

customers to offer something to. For example, we have about 15,000 preferred customers here at M.O.R.E., Inc, and we'll often invite all of them to do business with us or get involved in a new opportunity, a new project, or a new service. **So we're dealing with large numbers; and if in fact only 10% of our customers got involved with us on a particular project, that would be 1,500 people.** Even if we said we were looking for only 200, 300, or 500 people to get involved in something, while that would be a small percentage of our entire group of preferred customers, it's still a lot of people.

The number depends on your model—on what you're looking to accomplish. **But keep in mind that the number needs to be real.** If it's not, if you don't fulfill on your promises or it's obvious that you don't mean what you say, people will figure it out and you'll lose your credibility. **There's no real exclusivity if you say "this offer is only for *this* number of people," and it turns out that it's not.** So make it legit, based on your own numbers and your profit needs. Arrange things so that if you make the offer exclusive to 20 customers, you'll make more money in a week than you've made the entire month before. While you don't need to tell them that, you can't be shy about the number of people involved. **Make sure that they know how exclusive the offer truly is. When played right, this principal works wonderfully well—because it provides you with a psychological edge that most people simply can't resists.** You've made them feel like they've won when they grab that offer, like they've pulled one over on you and their friends and all the other poor slobs who didn't make it in... which means that you win, too. In the end, this can also give you the edge you need to do more business with them.

TOTAL SUCCESS!

The important thing to know is that you control the perceptions here, to a large degree—assuming they believe you, or know that they can trust you. You're the one who builds the value; you're the one who builds the exclusivity into your offers, making them more unique, more special, and seemingly less available to everybody else.

Start paying attention to how other marketers are doing this, because it doesn't just happen by accident. You can't just throw crap together and hope people will figure it out, like the guy did who sent me that impenetrable email this morning. As Nathaniel Hawthorne once said, "Easy reading is damn hard writing." **In other words, the more you work on it, the clearer it becomes.** So work hard on your copywriting, and do everything you can to build your offers so that you make your prospects feel special. That's surprisingly rare, as logical as it may seem; **very few marketers bother to make their prospects feel special.**

If you can do that effectively, you'll grab all the customers your competitors aren't getting—and you'll practically mint money.

CHAPTER THREE

"Business is a good game — lots of competition and a minimum of rules. You keep score with the money."

— *Nolan Bushnell*

Business as a Game

As you may recall, Atari was one of the first big computer game companies; it made money hand over fist back in the 1970s and early 1980s. This inspired the CEO and founder, Nolan Bushnell, to say, **"Business is a good game—lots of competition, and a minimum of rules. You keep score with money."** As a games purveyor, Bushnell knew what he was talking about. Atari has since passed from the scene, but it helped set the stage for all the other huge gaming companies that followed.

Bushnell was exactly right: **business *is* a game, and it's a great one at that.** I fully subscribe to this philosophy. I believe it should be an obvious point, too; but to most business people, it's apparently a secret they just can't fathom. They don't look at business as a game at all; it's more or less like a job to them. Well, I started my own business so that I could get away from that "job" mentality. I've always hated jobs. A job is where you work for somebody else, whereas when you have your own business, you work for *you*. Even when you play the game properly, surrounding yourself with the best and brightest people you can, and find the best vendors, suppliers, and joint venture partners possible… well, as the old saying goes, **"If it's meant to be, it's up to me." The responsibility all devolves to you, the person at the center of the business.**

TOTAL SUCCESS!

So it's best, I think, if you *do* see it as a game. **See it as something that's challenging, something that you play to win.** There are very few rules. Basically you have to avoid bankruptcy, avoid getting shut down by the government, avoid lawsuits, avoid getting overwhelmed by competitors, and, in general, avoid getting in any serious trouble... while making enough money to keep moving forward. **Use money to keep score, and make as much as you possibly can, so you can focus on the offensive side of the game, rather than the defense.** That's really the name of the game, because cash flow covers and overcomes a multitude of mistakes.

That said, I don't want to oversimplify business. It can be very complicated in numerous ways... which is one of the reasons why I love looking at business as a game. And, to me, it's a team sport. **You really do need to surround yourself with the very best players you possibly can, so you can delegate all your weaknesses and focus on the things you're best at.** Hopefully those things will include marketing and sales; if not, you'll need a business partner, or a joint venture business partner, who's tightly focused on both—because that's where all the money is to be made.

I'm often reminded of another of my all-time favorite quotes, which I memorized 15 years ago. I think of it often, especially when life and business get difficult. In his book *The Master Game*, Robert DeRopp said: **"Above all else, seek a game worth playing, and play it as if your entire life and sanity depended on it... for it does!"** I love that quote, and I hope you find some inspiration in it as well.

Business is a great game, full of challenges of all kinds.

You've got competitors trying to get a piece of your market segment at your expense. **You've got all kinds of market forces working constantly, subtly changing your marketplace.** You've got the government, which is constantly after you for this, that, and the other thing. **And by the way, all of us are in business with the government, whether we like it or not.** You can whine and cry about it, you can hate every minute of it... but it is what it is.

You'll have other challenges, too. Sometimes you have customer service issues, promotions that quit working, or supply issues. There are new problems all the time—problems, problems, and more problems. But that's life! Life is one continual series of ongoing problems, and there's no escape, no matter what you try. Anybody over the age of 40 who's not living in complete delusion *knows* this. **And yet, it's possible to reframe problems as if they're challenges, things that cause you to excel and force you to push harder.** In fact, you have to do that. You can't let problems take you down.

Seeing life as a challenge, and fighting unflaggingly against the problems you encounter, is all a part of that game mentality.

The best games are microcosms of life. I watched a really good football game recently, between two teams fighting for a place in the NFL playoffs. They both had the same record going into this game, and they're division rivals—so they really knew each other well, both offense and defense. It was a great game, a real battle, which made it a lot of fun to watch. You could see that some of the players were really frustrated; there was some fighting on the field, and they were trash talking each other at times. Both teams really wanted to win.

TOTAL SUCCESS!

Because so much was riding on this one game, the quarterback for New York was cracking jokes with his teammates all week, trying to get them to loosen up a bit, trying to get them to laugh and not to be nervous. **When you're nervous all the time, you've focused on the wrong things, and you can actually hurt yourself.** His team did lose; maybe that had something to do with it. In any case, it was a pretty close game until the very end.

You need to do what the New York quarterback did: **try to reframe your problems as challenges, face them with a sense of humor, and not let them get to you.** You're going to run into problems all the time. Life is problems, and business is amplified life. You get more of the good, sure, but you also get a whole lot more of the bad. I'm not trying to be negative here. Again, I want you to go into this with your eyes wide open, because you'll *need* to open your eyes and expect problems—so you can then try to solve as many of them you as can, as efficiently as you can. You especially need to solve the little problems before they become big ones.

Surround yourself with the very best people you can possibly find, and put them in areas where they offset your weaknesses—in order words, have them do all the things they're really good at that you're really bad at. **Then focus on keeping the whole thing running as best you can. Done right, it becomes a magnificent game.** Yes, it's difficult at times, and sometimes you go through some tough times; but that's when you develop your skills the most.

So don't let the bad times get to you—and they can, if you lose sight of the idea that this is all a big game. You hear stories

42

all the time about businesspeople who kill themselves, or die young because they just let the business get to them. I know people like that. There are businesspeople who are very close to me, whom I care deeply about, who are going through some damned tough times with their businesses. Things just aren't working out for them, and they're dealing with all kinds of problems—and they're letting it all get to them. **Well, you've got to learn to lighten up just to stay sane. You have to pull back a little, and refuse to take it all to heart.** You immobilize yourself if you let it get to you too much. If you're not fighting all the problems, obstacles, setbacks, and challenges along the way, **if you're not trying to look at them a little differently, then you become depressed... and then you can't perform, and then you're useless.**

We all have critics, and I'm no exception. Mine tell me I don't take things seriously enough. And I tell them they're wrong: **I take things *very* seriously, but I try not to let them get to me.** When you let these challenges build up, take them to heart, and allow them to beat you down, then you're incapable of performing to the level that you have to perform in order to solve those problems. **So it doesn't do you or anybody else any good to let all these things get to you. Consider them tests, because that's what they are:** they test your commitment, they help you build strength and character, and they help you sharpen your skills. It doesn't always feel good, but it's good for you.

You've heard it before: **you've got to keep your eyes on the prize.** Part of that process is focusing on marketing and sales, so you can keep your profits high—knowing that if you're focused on those things, then you're going to build those good habits that will get you through the bad patches. **Too many people just give up. They quit. You can't afford to let that happen to you.**

Let me reemphasize an important point that I've already made a number of times, because it's worth repeating: **I really believe that a company is a synergistic effort of talented people working together as a group.** You can surround yourself with good people who complement your skill-set, filling in the gaps where you're weak or simply lack certain knowledge and abilities. It's not always easy, and it doesn't always work smoothly, because whenever you bring people into a group you're bound to encounter all kinds of interpersonal problems. And yet, a truly effective organization works like clockwork—literally like all the gears and cogs in an old timepiece. Those little parts may all be of different sizes, and they may not be of equal importance; but if you remove one, the whole mechanism stops working. So you have to realize just how important your people are. **Surround yourself with the brightest, most trustworthy people you can find, and delegate to them all the functions you're weak in, or that they can do more cheaply.**

This works for all kinds of businesses. While every business is a reflection of the people at the top and the people who comprise it, and they serve various markets and all do things a little differently, nearly all businesses are alike at a very basic level. That is, they're all predicated on the same common denominators.

You see, there are only three ways to build any traditional

business. **First of all, you can make an effort to attract more customers.** There are all kinds of plays you can make within the business game to accomplish that one, and most businesspeople understand that. **The second thing you can do is encourage your existing customers to come back and buy more things.** If someone buys something from you once, do everything you can to get them to do business with you three or four times a year; and **then try to double their buying frequency to, say, six or eight times a year.** It's as simple as that, and there are plenty of strategies you can utilize to accomplish that end, too. The third thing you can do is get your customers to spend more money per transaction, so you can make a greater profit.

All three goals should be part of your grand marketing strategy, because when they're properly combined, the power of synergy comes into play. Start out by making yourself so exciting that people can't pass you by, and then stay so exciting that they not only never want to let you go, they're willing to give you more money every time they buy. Focus on those simple things. You'll still go through tough times—they're inevitable—but if you treat business as a game and follow these rules, you can make as much money as you want.

Now, when you get right down to it, the game is the same whether you're talking about business or an athletic event. Oh, the mechanics are different, but in both cases **it's all about doing your darnedest to dominate the competitors.** So Bushnell's characterization of business as a good game with lots of competition and minimal rules is appropriate; though I'll admit that it does oversimplify things in some ways. **The basic rules of the game may be simple, but they can be very broad**

and quite far-reaching.

Another thing that makes the business game different from a formalized sport is that the rules aren't all written down... and the rules that apply can depend on how you define your rulebook and playing field. **In some cases, the rules are more ethical than formal; and you have to tread very carefully when approaching those moral boundaries, which are not nearly as sharp as the lines on a football field or soccer pitch.** Ultimately, these are the rules that guide lives, not just a sport or a business... whereas in a game of football there are very specific rules that all the teams and all the players have to abide by during game time, but can ignore once they're off the field.

Then there are the government rule sets: laws and regulations that apply to an industry at large, and are very like the basic rules of a game. **But they're pliable, at least to some extent.** Some industries hire lobbyists to work with politicians, and try to acquire special favors so they don't have to play by the same exact rules that other businesses have to play by. And of course, **the rules you have to follow will vary to some extent depending on your industry.**

All that said, by and large the rules that we're governed by in business are fairly loose. You have a lot of freedom in how you operate, how you attract customers, and how you try to compete against the other people in your marketplace—so you can structure your business just about any way you want to, which actually gives you more leeway than many sports allow on the field of play. So while the analogy has its limitations, I think it's a valid one for a lot of reasons.

And when you play, you should play to win. Always. Chris Lakey recently came across an Internet blog written by the owner of the Dallas Mavericks, Mark Cuban, and brought it to my attention. Cuban started out as an entrepreneur; he struck it rich with the Initial Public Offering of an Internet startup, and then decided to buy a sports franchise. A lot of people admire him for both his business savvy and his enthusiasm as a sports fan. But in many ways, they're the same thing: he simply pays to win in both venues. Back in early 2005, Cuban laid out his philosophy in an entry called "The Sport of Business." For copyright reasons, I won't quote it extensively here; if you'd care to take a look (and I recommend you do), you can find it online at http://blogmaverick.com/2008/01/03/the-sport-of-business-2/.

One of things Cuban has to say—and, frankly, I think this captures his argument to a nutshell—is, **"The sport of business is the ultimate competition. It's 24x7x365 forever."** He's absolutely devoted to that game, and I think it shows in his success and in the fact that he was, in fact, able to purchase a sports franchise. I urge you to take a look at Cuban's blog—not just this entry, but others as well. You could certainly find worse businessmen to model yourself after.

Always play to win. One of our strategies here at M.O.R.E., Inc. is something we call "Ruthless Marketing," and I've written a few books on the subject, including *Ruthless Marketing* and *The Ruthless Marketing Attack*. **All the books in this series are about obtaining an unfair advantage in your marketplace by being an aggressive marketer—by going out there with a will to win, putting everything on the line, and (within moral and**

legal bounds) doing everything within your power to beat your competition. As Cuban points out in the blog entry I mentioned above, every day some stranger from somewhere in the world that you've never met is trying to come up with a way to put you out of business. That's what business competition is all about. It's *not* about making friends. It's not about getting together for tea or joining the local Chamber of Commerce so all the members can support each other in their efforts. That's great for some businesses, maybe; **but if you want to win, if you want that competitive edge, you've got to play at business like it's a sport that you're playing to win.**

If you're a professional ball player, you don't go out on the baseball field and say, "Well, I hope in the end it's a close game, and we win by one point. I hope they don't get their feelings hurt too bad when we do. I hope everyone can walk away happy, and feel like it was a good game." No, you want to put your boot on their neck and squeeze until they give it up! Think of it like the mixed martial arts or some forms of wrestling, where they basically fight until one of them can't go on anymore and just packs it in. You want to do that to your competitors. **You want to dominate them so much that they quit the game of business, because you're just so good at what you do.**

This is why people get so mad at businesses like Wal-Mart: because they come into a market and dominate it. Now, these people may claim they don't like Wal-Mart because the company doesn't pay fair wages, or it doesn't give its employees good enough health insurance; but the real reason they don't like Wal-Mart is because Wal-Mart is very, very good at what it does. **Wal-Mart dominates the market so hard that it drives other**

companies out of business. Sometimes the erstwhile competitors just give up without even trying when Wal-Mart or a similar competitor arrives on the scene. I've seen it happen.

But whether you think you have the capacity to succeed against a dominant force like Wal-Mart or not, **you have to** *try*. Otherwise, why bother to get into business and play the game in the first place? The aggressive attitude that Mark Cuban discussed in the abovementioned blog entry is exactly what it takes to win in the game of business. **You've** *got* **to be aggressive to win, because there's more competition than ever.** Ultimately, it's all about bringing new products to the marketplace, serving your customers, going to the wall full-bore, and being the best you can be so that, hopefully, you can win that game.

You can't let all the problems, petty issues, setbacks, and competition be your focus — or you'll end up going out of business, because you let the suffering overwhelm you. At some point, you'll decide that it just wasn't worth it to get into business for yourself, and you'll retire or go back to work for somebody else. **That's why you need to treat this as a game; a serious one, but a game nonetheless.** Accomplish everything you can by working within the rules; and when it's safe and moral to do so, push the envelope, just like a football or basketball player might do. They know the rules, but sometimes they step across the boundary... and sometimes they get called on it. Well, when that happens, or when something else goes wrong, they don't give up the game. They're playing to win; and so they move forward, doing the best they can to play successfully within those rules. And again, that's the way it is in business, too. **Don't let the rules get you down. There are some, but mostly they're rules you can live with.** Your main focus should be on winning the game of business by dominating your marketplace—which means you have to be the very best at whatever you do.

Back when Wal-Mart's founder, Sam Walton, was alive, nothing made him more upset than to hear the old rigmarole about how Wal-Mart was an unfair competitor, that it was ruining Main Street by killing off all the small businesses. He himself started as a small town merchant with a little Ben Franklin store. He had some problems with his landlord and other issues, and decided he needed to run his own company; and so he started Wal-Mart. Years later, he wrote a book called *Made In America;* and in that book, he devoted an entire chapter on ways to compete with Wal-Mart. **And you *can* compete! One of his best strategies was to shut down your Main Street location, then move your business as close as possible to the local Wal-Mart.** Essentially, he said, "Look, I'll bring you the traffic. People will come because I can give them a good selection for good prices." He emphasized that these things, along with convenience, are just about all that Wal-Mart offers. And think about it: sometimes, people do want more than just a good price, a good selection, and convenience.

But business owners sometimes forget this in the face of stiff competition... and as a result, they sometimes just fall apart or give up. Over in Hillsboro, Kansas, a small town of about 3,000-5,000 people, there used to be a Ben Franklin store on Main Street. It was there for decades. And then a little store chain called Alco, which is kind of like a miniature Wal-Mart, came to town and started scouting locations. Well, nine months before Alco even opened its doors in Hillsboro, the owner of the Ben Franklin folded his tent suddenly and went out of business. When I asked him why, he said, "I can't compete with Alco." And I responded, "But Alco isn't even opening for another nine months!" It just was ridiculous; I couldn't believe it. **He deprived his community of his services, and himself of a profit, because he didn't want to even try to compete with Alco.** That's no way to play... but that's exactly what far too many people do. They give up far too early.

I've got a close family member who did something like this: she had a business, and she gave it up too soon. She quit after less than two years, and that was over 10 years ago. She's gone through some serious financial struggles since. **But I believe that if she hadn't just given up, her business would probably be thriving right now.** I believe that business would be phenomenally profitable, in fact, because she had everything going for her; she just wasn't willing to ride out the tough times. If she'd kept at it, by now she would have had a business other people would have envied. But she quit. She gave up.

There's no such thing as failure—except in giving up. That's when you truly fail. Everything else is just a speed bump on the road to success.

If you're going to play the game, **play it to win.**

CHAPTER FOUR

The Power of Focus...

**Don't spend your time
managing problems.
Spend your time building
your opportunities.**

The Power of Focus

Don't spend all your time managing problems. **Instead, spend your time building opportunities.**

So many businesspeople do nothing but put out brushfires all day, because they try to personally manage every little problem that comes along. That's a mistake; you need to get other people to do that. Train your employees to handle most of their own problems, and arrange things so that anything left over goes straight to someone who specializes in fixing problems. That way, you can narrow your focus like a laser beam, and devote all your time to building your business.

I've got a sign on my wall that displays a quote from a certain marketing expert, someone who's helped us an awful lot here at M.O.R.E., Inc. It goes like this: **"Distractions abound. You must fight for focus."** There will always be hordes of little problems fighting for your attention, from the time you get up in the morning to the time you lay your head down at night. I've got another quote up on my wall close to that one, and it's from the famous French revolutionary, Victor Hugo: "Those who live are those who fight." I translate that to business-speak so that it reads, **"Those businesses that survive are those that fight." And you've *got* to fight! You can never give up.** The minute you give up is the minute you lose that fight. You've got to fight for focus!

TOTAL SUCCESS!

Previously, I outlined the only three effective techniques for building a business: **you attract customers, you get those people to buy from you more often, and you increase the average transaction size to build your profit margins when they do come back.** Those are the three things you really need to fight to focus on. And right off the mark, you have to realize that your competitors are after those same people you're after. Therefore, those competitors are your enemies. While it's good, from a political standpoint, to hobnob with these people at Chamber of Commerce meetings and such, never lose sight of the fact that they're trying to take business away from you. You can extend that to a regional and national perspective as well. **There are only so many good customers out there, and everybody is looking for those people.**

How do you attract those customers? You've got win them over. They're not just going to come to you, so you've got to find ways to *get* them to come to you. **This means you need to really get inside their heads and hearts, and become them to some extent.** Get behind their eyeballs; think like they think. Who are they? What do they want more than anything else? How can you give that to them better than all your competitors? **What can you do that gives them what they want the most that nobody else is giving them?**

Usually, those aren't questions you're going to be able to answer quickly; and most likely, any answers that pop into your head easily aren't especially good answers. They're answers that might lead to *better* answers, but this isn't about just trying to come up with quick solutions. **You've really got to focus tightly on this and put some thought into it.** *Fight* for that

focus. What are your biggest competitors doing that you're *not* doing? What is your biggest competitive advantage, and how can you exploit it more? These are things you need to think very, very deeply about.

How can you attract the attention of the people in the marketplace, and steal customers from your competitors? Once you have them, how do you hold onto them, and get them to come back for more—so that they keep spending money with you? What kind of new products and services can you develop to do that, and how can you come up with new stuff all the time? **And remember, the money you want next month or next quarter has to come from something you're working on today, which is why you've got to be innovating constantly.** If you can't or don't want to develop those new products and services today, there are all kinds of joint venture relationships you can get involved with, all kinds of products and services out there that you can license. How you handle this is only limited by your imagination—which is the good news and the bad news, I suppose.

Finally: how can you increase the size of your average transaction? How can you maximize that profit margin? You have to get inventive here, because none of this is easy. **But the fact that it's challenging is what makes a vibrant, growing, changing business so absolutely, positively fulfilling.** You'll experience some frustration, some tough times, and sometimes you may want to quit; but a constant focus on maximizing your profit, and the benefits that result, will prove to you how temporary such things are.

So whenever you get overwhelmed, when the frustration

and the confusion becomes too great, go back to the basics— those three ways to build a business—and remember that it's all about selling more products and services to more people, more often, for more profit per transaction, with greater efficiency. **That's the formula. Write that down and hang it on your wall so you can see it every day.** Think about it deeply; because each one of those things I just described requires a focused strategy to achieve. Consistently work *on* your business, not *in* your business. **Spend the majority of your work time focusing on getting more people to give you more money.**

This can be a real challenge, and no doubt you'll find yourself struggling from time to time with how to gain clarity for the mission and for whatever you're trying to accomplish. **"Those who live are those who *fight*."** Don't lose sight of that.

Recently, Chris Lakey shared a story with me about a family adopting this little girl from Russia; he said when his wife showed him a picture of this little girl, he thought she looked about two years old, tops. But it turned out she was nine—which Chris found shocking. She looks like a baby, so obviously she's been very malnourished and neglected, the victim of a major tragedy. But she survived; and she's here now in the States, getting treatment and putting on weight. Hopefully, she'll recover and have a great future. When Chris first saw this little girl, his first thought was, **"That's a fighter."** Given what she's gone through, she might have died long ago; but she fought to survive. Now, there's a fighter for you!

This little girl can teach us all a valuable lesson. **You see, in business you have to fight too; and the way you fight is to focus tightly on the things that really, truly matter.** It's too easy to get bogged down in all the little things that don't help you achieve your goals—so caught up in the day-to-day minutia of running your business that you never stop and do anything to improve it. **Well, if you've got to obsess on something, obsess on building opportunities for your business. Stop wasting time on managing problems.** Every business has them, inevitably, since everything that's worth doing has its challenges, setbacks, and things that generally don't go right. They can be monumental distractions that really put you off your game, draining the focus and energy you need to build your business—if you let them.

If you're always putting out fires, it doesn't take too much to blow an entire day. We all have days like that. It's just a matter of whether those are the norm for you, or the exception. **It may seem like an oxymoron, but it's not uncommon to get so busy that you never really do anything.** In my case, I can get mobbed by people asking for a minute here, a minute there, stopping me in the hall, calling me with a question, sending me little emails... and I can spend all day doing things that accomplish nothing in terms of achieving our overall business goals. Oh, those things probably needed to get done and, in some cases, I was the only one who could do them, **but they kept me from focusing on important things.**

On the other hand, on some days I don't do more than a few things; but those are sometimes my most productive days. There are times when I do little more than spend a lot of time on the phone, with Chris Lakey for instance, but we spend our time brainstorming and talking about ideas that will hopefully result in future profits. **Quantity has its own value, as they say, but**

quality tends to be more profitable, at least in terms of how you direct your time. It's worth doing only a few things in a day when those things are very productive in terms of bringing in more sales and profits.

So focus on the mission at hand, and be single-minded in your approach to your ultimate goals. Small business owners tend to be hampered by their inclination to wear all the hats in the business; and we all struggle with this to some degree. You see this with service industry especially, where the businessman is often his own bookkeeper, sets his own appointments, does all his own marketing, and handles collections on top of doing all the actual work. Ultimately, all this keeps him from bringing in more business, because he can't focus on just that one thing. Worse, because he's doing all those things at once, it probably means he's doing none of them well. The temptation here is that that's the best way to do it, because you don't have to pay anybody else—but often, **there's a benefit to paying someone to do something that you could do yourself. It frees you up to become more valuable to your business.**

In the end, you'll spend *less* money to get those things done, because your labor is worth so much. Let's say that your direct efforts in your business earn you $100 an hour when you really focus on what matters. Well, if you're spending time doing something that someone else could do for $15 an hour, then essentially you're giving up $85 an hour by doing it yourself. Does that make any sense to you?

Now, if you enjoy doing something, fine—but do it in your spare time as a hobby. You may like to dabble in web design, for example, and maybe eventually you could build and manage your own website. **Still, you should never consider it as anything more valuable to you than, say, golf.** There's nothing necessarily wrong with golfing, but if golfing keeps you from accomplishing your business goals, then you need to limit the amount of time you spend on the golf course.

You have to prioritize your time. We all have the same 24 hours in a day, and some of that is going to be spent sleeping, eating, commuting, and doing all the other things we have to do on a day-to-day basis. There are only so many potentially productive hours to spend on business; and if you can make $100 an hour by focusing like a laser on your business goals, then how can you justify spending four work hours on golf... or on building a website that a web designer could build for $50 an hour, or less?

Don't waste your time managing problems or doing things that other people can do just as well for less money. *Do* **spend your time building opportunities and working on the tasks that bring in the most revenue:** tasks like attracting more customers, getting your existing customers to come back more often, and increasing the average size of each transaction. Spend more of your time thinking about those things, and less time doing low-dollar tasks, and you'll find that your productivity will increase. **You'll also find yourself having more ideas and creating more opportunities for yourself.**

That's the power of focus. Consider the visual analogy of just being out in the sun. A few minutes of exposure aren't going to hurt you; in fact, it's healthy to get out in the sun a little. But if you stay out too long, you can get a nasty sunburn—and if you bring a magnifying glass out on a bright day, you can focus it in such a way as to burn a hole right through a piece of paper. **A good business focus is like that; and you can really put it to work burning away the dross. So don't let yourself be diverted by all the distractions that hinder so many other businesspeople.** Get serious about doing what you do best, and let other people do what they do best.

The truth is, even if you *can* do something better than anyone else, it's probably still worth it to hire someone else to do it if they can do it more cheaply than you can. **Keep only thing the high value stuff that you can do best, especially the marketing and innovation.** It's as simple as that... even if it's not always easy.

CHAPTER FIVE

The best marketing is <u>always</u> in a constant state of flux.

The Best Marketing is Always in a State of Flux

This business life is unavoidably confusing... so you have to adapt to that reality, and harness the power of constant change.

So many of the people that we try to help here at M.O.R.E., Inc. are just running around confused and frustrated most of the time. They have no idea know what to do next. Sometimes, they've got so many ideas they simply don't know where to begin; they don't know which ideas are the best, and they're paralyzed by that fact. They sometimes spend years frozen in this state, accomplishing nothing. **Well, as we like to point out, you've really got to learn on the job. Just jump into the fray and start swinging.** You'll start figuring the basic moneymaking methods over time; and once you develop a customer base and the money starts rolling in, it becomes infinitely easier.

If you have a customer base—that is, people who like you, trust you, and have bought from you before—then those people are already pre-conditioned to buy from you again. In fact, they *want* to buy from you again! They'd much rather do business with you than with someone that they don't know, don't like, and don't trust. **So once you earn somebody's trust, you're doing them a serious disservice if you're not trying to re-sell them things similar to the types of things they bought from** you before.

And while those new things have to be very similar in many respects to the things you've already sold them, they do have to be different. I know that's a little confusing on the face of it; what I mean is that you have to offer your customers things that have new twists and improvements, but simultaneously provide some familiarity, some of the same features they enjoyed before. **Understand that customers are addicted to the new, so they always want something different... but it can't be *too* different.** Many times, they just want a veneer of newness... and your job is to serve that up to them.

To truly succeed at business, you need to keep your marketing moving and changing all the time. **In the race to retain customers, you have to continually pay attention to them, insuring that there's always something new, something different, something *next* in your queue.** We've taken that to heart here at M.O.R.E., Inc. In fact, I've got a little sign hanging on my wall that simply says, "Do what's next." I'm always looking for that next thing—and you have to do so as well.

The truth is, your customers will almost always be willing to buy far more from you than you'll be able to produce for them (though there are exceptions to the rule). I used to spend a lot of time worrying that I was selling too much stuff to our customers too often, but I've never seen any evidence of that actually happening. Now I worry about just the opposite—that we *don't* offer our customers enough. **That's why we're constantly re-selling to our existing customer base. It's the key to getting rich—and it's a big part of what successful marketing is all about.**

Here's a great quote for you: **"Whatever is revolutionary is evolutionary."** By that, I simply mean that you need to be constantly incorporating the things that have worked the best for you in the past into anything new that you're offering your customers. And how do you find out what works? By running it up the flagpole and seeing who salutes. As I've mentioned, some of our clients spend years in a full-fledged paralysis of analysis, so confused that they never even figure out how to get started. **Well, you can't plan out everything ahead of time—so you just have to get started.** And here's the thing: once you do get started, you can't expect to get things right every time. In fact, even when you do have a customer base, and you have a good sense of what those people like, you're still going to end up confused sometimes. You're never going to escape that.

Confusion is an inevitable part of the creative process, along with frustration and pressure. And you don't really want to escape these things completely anyway, because **some confusion and frustration is essential to creativity. Many of your best ideas will come when you're under the gun.** You don't have to stay stuck in that paralysis of analysis. **Constantly test new things, so you *can* find out what works best, and then incorporate those elements into your next test.** You only need to have major breakthroughs every once in a great while. As long as you've got a group of customers who trust you, like you, and appreciate you, they'll do business with you again and again.

There are other factors in the equation, of course, but **good marketing essentially boils down to attraction and retention. And the best marketing is always in a state of flux,** because you're always searching for things that work better. You're constantly experimenting, constantly testing, always looking for something new that your customers will get excited about. And one thing always does lead to another, so you have to step out in faith and figure everything out as you go along. You can't try to get it all right from the word go.

I empathize deeply with our customers and clients who are confused about the best route to take. I understand what that's all about. It can be very frustrating—almost like trying to put together a 5,000-piece jigsaw puzzle that someone's thrown on the ground and mixed up. You're thinking, *How the devil am I going to join all these tiny pieces into a coherent picture?* Well, you start with the corners; that's fairly easy, once you find them. Then you put the edges together—the frame, if you will. Then you keep matching patterns and shapes. **The more pieces you get together, the easier it becomes; and toward the end it becomes very simple, doesn't it?** If you've ever put together a jigsaw puzzle, you know exactly what I'm talking about. By the time you've got 80% of those pieces together, the rest snap into place pretty easily.

It's the same thing with making money. You're very confused in the beginning, so you start hunting for the corners and edges. But some people never find them, so they never escape from that state of confusion... and they may eventually give up in response. **You have to realize that in business, the corners and edges of the jigsaw puzzle involve developing a customer base that you can then focus on serving.** Offer your customers more of what they bought from you before; develop new twists that make those items attractive again; look around and see what your competitors are doing well. **Then**

take the best of the best of what you end up with, and work it into everything you offer. Leave out the weaker elements, and whatever just doesn't take off, and you'll make your new offers stronger.

Here's a good example. We're working on a promotion right now that we call "the EOP-4 promotion"— and I won't even tell you what "EOP" stands for, because it just doesn't matter in this context. Suffice it to say that it's a fourth generation product; that is, this is the fourth time we've incorporated EOP into an offer. We made $140,000 on EOP-4 in our first two days of sales. **EOP-4 is so powerful because we've combined nine different elements, all based on the best-of-the-best of what we've done recently.** If somebody takes just one of those pieces, they get the other eight for free. It's all packaged with a proven type of promotion that's worked for us before. Will we have an EOP-5? I can't say for sure that we will, but it wouldn't surprise me if we do.

We have another promotion we call IAMS. Again, I won't say what it stands for, because it's just not necessary for this example; **but we're on our tenth generation of IAMS in about six years.** Some of those generations have involved relatively minor improvements on the previous generations. If it worked before it'll work again, so we're just changing little bits and pieces. **Again, it's got a veneer of newness; but behind it is something that's been proven to work for us many times.**

We've been taking advantage of this general concept since the late 1980s, when we started with a program called "Dialing for Dollars." We kept expanding and improving it, making it better in various ways, so that we ended up with four different

69

versions of "Dialing for Dollars" before the promotion died out. And we still use elements from that same promotion today, a couple of decades later.

Probably our best example of a multi-generation product originated back in the mid-1990s, when the World Wide Web first took over and made the Internet accessible for non-techno geeks like myself. We were already heavily involved with electronic marketing; but back then it was something called Computer Bulletin Boards, which many people have never even heard of nowadays. **In any case, we were already very much engaged in helping our clients make money through electronic marketing. Then, BOOM! All of a sudden the World Wide Web came along.**

We were there in the right place at the right time with the right people who had the right plan, and money poured in faster than we knew how to intelligently spend it. We just blew millions of dollars; I wish I had some of that money now. **But the point is, those millions came raining down on our heads because, again, we incorporated the best elements of something that was already working very well for us into something that was new and different.**

What is revolutionary is evolutionary. The revolutionary evolves out of all the things that worked well for you before; you're simply incorporating the best of the best of those elements into your new products and services, always keeping things in flux, because your customers constantly want something new. The best marketing is constantly changing, flowing like an active river that cuts out a path in its valley, moving back and forth so that it looks different now than it did 20 years ago—and it'll look different yet again 20 years from now.

This constant flux can be daunting to think about, because we like things to be constant. We like to have things we can rely on; when something is in a state of constant change, we can't tackle it quite as easy, and so it may be scary. **But I think it's important to also remember that while your marketing must be in flux, and the technology can change, your marketplace is more fixed.** That's what you need to focus on. The market you serve will, for the most part, stay the same.

Now, over the decades, marketplaces do evolve. For example, the mail order industry has changed quite a bit in the last 25 years or so, especially since the Internet became so prominent. Businesses that didn't at least account for the Internet soon learned the error of their ways. Some went out of business as a result, because when you stick your head in the sand and pretend something new doesn't exist, you still have to deal with the consequences. **One of the consequences of the Internet is the fact that most of your customers are now online to some degree, and they expect *you* to be there.**

The Internet has also changed the way we deliver content, especially in the information publishing industry. Before the Internet, if you wanted to sell an information course of some kind, you might deliver it in a three-ring binder or, later, on CD or DVD; and certainly that kind of content still exists today. **But a lot of businesses have started delivering content directly online.** Often, you can now download a digital version of a book to your computer so you don't need to wait for the hard copy. **You can even download audio and video, or stream it online.** Also, there's a lot more free content online.

TOTAL SUCCESS!

Whereas people used to have to buy things to really feel like they were getting solutions, now you can get many of those solutions for the price of the time it takes to navigate to a website. In some cases, you might have to give up an email address or a name to get on somebody's e-mailing list, but that's essentially all you have to pay.

Has that changed the way mail order marketers do business? Absolutely! **So the marketplace has, in fact, evolved in some ways... but at the most basic level, it's still the same.** It's still made up of the same people with the same needs, so there are always fixed things there that you can focus on that make it easier to reach that marketplace, even though the methods you use to reach those customers may be (and must be) in a constant state of flux. Buyers are still buyers. It doesn't matter whether they're buying online or offline or by email or snail mail; whatever the case, they're customers in that marketplace for a reason. **They're responsive within that marketplace because of some psychological factor that's made them want or need to be a part of that marketplace.** Those things don't change, even though the marketplace may evolve as a whole over years and decades.

Let's say you're a golfer. Golf itself has evolved over the years, and the equipment is a bit different now than it was a few decades ago; but mostly the people who are struggling with their golf games are the same kinds of people who struggled with their games 10 years ago, 20 years ago, or 30 years ago. They're still looking for some edge that will help them beat their buddies on the golf course. **So the psychology behind the marketplace is basically the same,** even though the drivers are bigger now, the putters are different, and the golf balls have evolved.

It's the same thing in our market, the moneymaking market. We've been involved in this marketplace for more than 20 years, and people are still looking to make extra money. **Even though the way they respond or the kinds of things they buy in this marketplace might change over time, the *reasons* why people buy pretty much stay the same.** Sometimes people are looking to supplement their income for one reason or another; for example, a woman might want to work at home so she can more easily care for her new baby. Another client might be a middle-aged man who wants to retire and spend more time with his spouse, or who wants to travel—so he's looking for some kind of a business that gives him more flexibility. Perhaps the prospective customer is just flat broke, and looking for anything that could make them a little bit of money—any kind of job or part-time business on the side.

So there are all kinds of reasons why people enter the marketplace; and those haven't really changed over the years, even though the ways that people respond have. Perhaps they're looking for more information online than offline these days, and maybe they're looking for an information product that they can download quickly, or an audio program they can listen to on their iPod. But the reasons they're buying— the psychology behind it—hasn't really changed much.

That's how it works with a lot of marketplaces. The people within it are the constants; so you can focus on those constants, resting assured in the knowledge that the people you're offering your products and services to don't change much. The marketing, though—than changes constantly, because it must.

TOTAL SUCCESS!

Never forget that the best marketing is always in a state of flux. You're always busy, always tweaking and testing; and it really is like a jigsaw puzzle that you constantly have to work on, following the clues in the marketplace to piece the picture together. Unfortunately, that picture isn't *entirely* fixed; it does gradually change... which is one of the reasons that *you* need to keep changing and adapting. **In the end there may be all kinds of different pieces involved, representing all your changing marketing plans, but it's a solvable puzzle if you keep working at it.**

The more you focus on the customers in your marketplace, the closer you'll come to completing that puzzle. You'll start seeing how the pieces fall together, seeing how things work in conjunction with or in relation to each other; and you'll be able to change along with that overall picture as the pieces subtly change. Just keep your eye on the ultimate goal of making a profit by serving that marketplace in all the things you do, and try not to get distracted. And realize that it's not *exactly* like completing a puzzle; when you get right down to it, there's no completing a puzzle of business. It's a constant flow, with pieces coming and going, with some even disappearing after you've placed them, and there are always new challenges to wrestle with. **But you do see the model take shape as you serve your customers and as you see profits come in—as you see satisfied people moving into and out of your business life.**

All the marketing you do—that constant ebb and flow of attracting customers by running ads, promoting local events, and just getting your brand out there in front of people's eyes—is all a part of this ever-changing puzzle. **The marketing is part of** the reason the business puzzle is never static; it can't be.

You should constantly be analyzing your marketing results, and trying to find ways to improve them. One of the worst things you can do is just let your advertising work without trying to measure it or otherwise determine whether it's doing any good for you. **You can't just keep your ads the same from one year to the next unless you know they're bringing in the money.** If they are, your only changes should be tweaks to see if you can make them even more effective; if they're not, then you definitely need to try something new. Try to figure out why you're not getting the number of customers through your door that you'd like, or why you're not making the money you hoped to make.

If your advertising is stale, it probably means your customers are stale. They're probably bored with your marketing message. Think about how you react when you see the same TV commercial over and over again... eventually you tune it out, right? So if your advertising isn't changing—i.e., if you're not refreshing the things you're doing to attract and retain customers—they're probably getting bored with you. I'm sure the results you're getting in your business will speak to that as well.

The changes required to shake up your results may be amazingly simple, and can relate to just about anything about your product. In retail sales, it could come down to changing the product's name, changing the size of the box, or adding "new and improved" to the sales copy (assuming that's true, of course). Or think of restaurants. Restaurants are always adding new things to the menu that are similar to what they already offer; and you know, there's not really that much new in the food industry. There's some room for creativity, but a burger is a burger. Still, they'll doctor it up and tell you it's some super-duper fancy burger now, because it's got three pieces of meat on it and two pieces of cheese, and maybe it's got jalapenos and bacon on top of that lettuce and tomatoes and pickles and onion.

Some burger joints offer something like 30 different kinds of hamburgers. Well, they're all mostly the same, with just minor differences; but they keep the menu changing, and they often come up with a new burger of the week or the month. They've always got something new they're rolling out, like the way McDonalds will bring the McRib back and then it'll go away for a while, replaced by a new sandwich. **They do all these things not because the new product necessarily tastes that different, but because they've got to have a reason to keep you coming in.** If you find out the McRib is back, you might want to go grab one. If you find out they're playing Monopoly at McDonalds, which they do a couple times a year, you might want to go back in. Or if you find out they've added another kind of salad and you're into salads, maybe you'll go check it out.

They're constantly changing things to keep you coming back to do business with them. Otherwise, you might get bored. If they never changed the menu, and the look of the restaurant was always the same, if nothing was ever any different, eventually it would get stale. The customers would dry up, and they'd end up going out of business. That's the way it is with all kinds of businesses. **The marketing simply has to be in a state of flux, because that's what the customers demand.**

You need to give your customers what they want, or you're out of business. Period. So while the market*place* is fixed, to a degree, never forget that your market*ing* can never be if you expect to be successful.

Success is a moving target, so you constantly have to keep readjusting your aim. **Yet basic human nature does not change; as they say, "The more things change, the more they remain the same."** I love that quote, because it means that there are some things that you can count on. But it's not true across the board; people are fascinated by the new. For example, there may be only so many ways to cook and serve pizza—it's just dough, sauce, cheese, and a few toppings—but even pizza consumers want to see something new on a regular basis. Some of the stuff you see in the commercials looks pretty stupid, but they're doing it for this reason. They *have* to come up with new stuff in order to entice the customer; and this holds true whatever you happen to be selling.

People want new products, all the time... so serve them up! If you don't give them the new, someone else will. Stay focused on the big picture, but keep your marketing in flux. **Incorporate the best of the best of what's worked in the past into your new products, but always test and try new things as well.** Constantly keep this mind. Any time you become too frustrated or too confused, go right back to this goal, and it'll help keep you on track.

CHAPTER SIX

Most people are secretly looking for someone to lead them by the hand.

Most People are Secretly Looking for Someone to Lead Them by the Hand

Consumers are confused these days, more so than ever before. They don't know what to do. There are too many choices, too many decisions. There are too many competitors in the marketplace, all shouting and screaming at once. Too many promises are being made to them; there are too many different products and services to choose from... and it's all too much. They're just overloaded.

As a result, most consumers become frustrated and extremely skeptical—in fact, many move beyond skeptical to cynical. Now they don't believe anything. They're not going to be taken advantage of, by God! Of course, those people still buy products and services. **They're looking for someone to lead them by the hand and tell them what to do, so they respond very well to a confident salesperson or a very enthusiastic sales message.**

That goes back to what I was saying in the last principle, about how the more things change the more they remain the same. **People have always been influenced by enthusiasm—** they love somebody who says, "Hey, follow me!" in a very confident, enthusiastic way, especially if that person is making all kinds of promises. **Charisma really sells; people have and will always respond to that, because it's part of human nature.**

The more confused and frustrated people are, the more

they're looking for someone to tell them exactly what to do; someone they can follow, someone they can believe in. So that's what you need to aim for with your marketing. Admittedly, that's easy to say, but not always easy to learn; so one of the best ways to learn how to do this is by studying what other people are already doing. **Which people are making the most money in your marketplace? They're not doing it by accident**—and they're probably not going to tell you how they're doing it, even if they understand it themselves. Essentially, it's up to you to decipher what they're doing to create these irresistible offers that compel people to give them money.

Pay special attention to the ones serving the same basic markets you want to serve. **Get on their customer lists, and spend some money with them in the name of research.** Pull back; be objective. Buy, but don't allow yourself to get emotionally involved in their sales methods. This allows you to look at the subject in the most objective way possible, so you can find out how they're getting people to take action in spite of all of the confusion, frustration, skepticism, and cynicism in the marketplace. I've already described some of the methods they use. One is simply extreme confidence.

There's one fellow we often do business with who's got this one down pat. We'll conduct seminars where as many as nine speakers come together to pitch their various products and services, and sometimes this gentleman outperforms all the others combined. People scratch their heads and wonder, "Oh, my God, what's he doing?" They think that he's got some kind of magical sales ability... and in a way, he does. The customers love him, because, well, he's lovable. **They're attracted to him because he's attractive. He's extremely confident. He carries himself**

in such a way that you would never *not* trust him. He looks the part, he plays the part, and he's exactly what he appears to be; otherwise, he wouldn't be coming to our events. We wouldn't be doing business with him if he weren't an honorable man. **He inspires that trust, that confidence, which people crave.** They naturally want to follow him because he's so absolutely confident about what he's doing, and he does a great job of answering all the biggest objections they have. He sells them without them realizing they've been sold while he's up on the stage doing his magic. He's got it down as an art form by now.

A lot of marketers are like this gentleman I'm talking about. These pitch people make millions promoting various products and services because it *is* an art form with them. **They've been doing it a long time and they've perfected it; they take the best of the best of everything that's worked for them before, and keep incorporating that into every new project or service they sell.** It's a skill set they continue to develop; and as their skills improve, their moneymaking ability improves along with them. Which is not to say that they aren't genuine; some may be hucksters, but the best of them are honestly enthusiastic about what they sell. **You have to be, because honest enthusiasm infects others.**

I wish somebody had told me 20 years ago what I'm telling you now. I wish they had said, "Hey, T.J., these are *skills*. All the things you have to do to get tens of thousands of people to give you millions of dollars are skills that have to be developed over time. **And you *can* develop those skills if you'll just get started, study what other people are doing, try to emulate them as much as possible, don't give up, and keep trying new things.**" If somebody had drilled that into my head, it would have saved me a lot of problems—so I'm hoping that my telling you these things in this book will help *you*.

Again, when somebody's making money steadily, it's not happening by accident. **There are combinations of things they're doing that cause people to give them all that money.** The persuasive power of a confident salesperson or message, their enthusiasm, is a necessary part of it. But another part is something I touched on earlier: answering people's biggest objections. **You need to isolate their greatest fears, and have ready answers for their skepticism and cynicism. You need to clearly tell people what they're going to get.** Paint that picture, make them want it, and present them with offers that are very much benefit-driven. People don't care as much about the features of a product or service as they do the benefits. **The benefit is the emotional reward they receive when they buy it. That's what they're really looking for.**

They're also looking for certainty. The more hectic life gets, and the more things are competing for and screaming for their attention, the more they need something they can count on. They're confused; they're frustrated; they're cynical; they're skeptical. **So the more you can give them something in a way that communicates certainty, the better off you are.** Because that's what people are looking for: certainty in an uncertain world. **Tell them exactly what they're going to get, explain the biggest benefits... and make sure they know exactly what's going to happen if they say no.** Towards the end of your sequence, after you've already made them additional follow-up offers again and again and tried to get them to respond, start explaining what might happen to them if they *don't* respond. Now you're playing into their fears, in such a way that they're thinking, "Holy crap, I'd better at least check this out!"

Beyond that, build as much risk reversal as you possibly can into your offers. **And what is risk reversal? It's simply where you stack all of the risk on your side of the table, so they have none at all.** You let people take action without any possibility of losing. **You assure them they're going to get their money back if your offer isn't everything you said it was, or if it's not perfect for them.** If they're even the slightest bit unhappy in any way—or for no reason at all—they can get out if they want to. You make it very, very easy for them to say yes, and very, very, *very* hard for them to say no.

All that makes a lot more sense when you study how other people in the field are doing it, and actually see these ideas that I'm talking about in action. So don't just read through this and forget it. Study your subject, find out how other marketers are handling things, and then emulate what they're doing.

You can't be too overt about setting yourself up as a leader, by the way. **Remember that most people are *secretly* looking for someone to lead them by the hand.** They don't want to flat-out admit it. If you were to ask a thousand people, "Do you like to be led, or are you a leader?", I think most would lie to themselves (and you), saying that they're leaders. And yet, the evidence points to the exact opposite, a fact that's obvious to the savvy observer. You'll see that if you put on your psychologist's cap and do some people watching. Smart marketers key on this point and use it to their advantage.

Kansas has a really nice State Fair, and it happens to be held close to where we live. Chris Lakey tries to get over there once a year and do some people watching, because it's interesting and instructive to see how folks behave in such an environment. **The one thing you see over and over again is that most people want to do what everybody else is doing.** I think this starts at an early age, with the whole peer pressure issue. People want to be seen as popular; they want to be seen as going with the flow. A lot of people won't tell you that, no matter how true it may be. They'll tell you they want to be leaders, and they'll tell you they're original... but they show themselves to be anything *but* original through their actions.

Even people who consider themselves nonconformist or "fringe" are like this. Take the skateboard crowd, or the Goths. Both groups like to consider themselves outsiders, or somehow original... and they're anything but. You'll notice that they all dress alike and act the same way. By and large they're followers, really.

The simple fact of the matter is that most people want someone to tell them what to do. Look at the popular TV shows, or the popular music. There's a reason they're popular; they're easy to watch or listen to and, frankly, few people are going to fault you for being a fan of a Top 40 artist or this week's #1 TV show. For the same reason, if you wear the popular brand of clothing, no one is going to ask why. Generally speaking, you can blend in with everybody else.

If you *really* want to be an outsider, try saying that you listen to some obscure band that no one else has heard of... or if they do know about them, they think their music is weird. Or try to be out there on the fringe of political thought, and see if you don't get chastised. Look at the candidates for political office in recent years who haven't at least pretended to be mainstream thinkers. They don't do well, because they're not part of the mob, like all the other politicians. **People out there on the edge have trouble gaining a following.**

As you work on your marketing, you need to stay keenly aware of this phenomenon as well, so you can use it to your advantage. **Yes, people need to know that you're worthy of being a leader, but you also have to make it easy for them to follow you.** Realize, too, that most people prefer a strong leader. They're looking for someone who will step up and guide them through whatever scenario they find themselves in—whether you're talking business, politics, or religion. **In your marketplace, that means they want you to provide the solutions they need to their problems, whether that's excess weight, hangnails, or tips on making more money.**

We've all had to consult experts on specific topics. **These are cases where we've deliberately sought out a leader to tell us what to do and, in some cases, to take charge and do our tasks for us.** Right now, Chris Lakey is preparing to start a non-profit organization, and he doesn't know a whole lot about non-profit law or accounting. He's learning, of course, but for the moment he's consulting a professional who deals with those kinds of things, so he can make sure he's proceeding correctly. He needs guidance on which documents to file with the state to get a non-profit corporation set up, and he needs help applying for a non-profit tax status as a 501(c)(3) corporation, so people who donate to his organization can get a tax deduction for doing so. So he's using an attorney whom he feels is an expert on this, and will be able to help him make sure he gets it done right. **He is, in this instance, deliberately choosing to be led by**

someone who knows how to do what he needs done. Sure, he might be able to figure some of it out on his own; but he really doesn't want to take the time or risk making mistakes.

That's really what people want in all marketplaces, at all levels. Now, there are always some things an individual consumer can lead himself or herself in, so they don't need any help. Chris is that way with computers; but someone who doesn't know computers very well might well be looking for a leader in that area if they need help. You may have seen commercials or ads where the computer professionals purport to be experts. Perhaps you've talked to some people who've used a particular company, and they've had good experiences. You know this company is a leader in computer repair in your area... so you go to them because they *are* experts. You know they are because they've told you so, not just through their advertising but also word-of-mouth—both word and deed, if you will.

For as long as I can remember, one of our marketing friends has called himself "America's foremost Internet marketing consultant." Well, is he? I don't know; maybe there's someone better than him, and maybe there isn't. But he calls himself that, so I tend to believe it; and his marketplace certainly responds to him that way. They consider him *the* expert in Internet marketing... and the fact is, it's a title that he gave himself. **He's put himself out there as a leader, and so he *is* a leader within the marketplace of people who are looking to be Internet marketers themselves.**

And let me re-emphasize that people *secretly* want to be led, because again, most people just aren't willing to admit it— even to themselves. **By and large, we just want someone to**

follow. Some people actually want to be in second place; that way, they still have someone telling them where to go and what to do... but some of the glory rubs off on them when things go right. If things go south, the second banana can always blame the leader for steering them in the wrong direction.

The unvarnished truth is that there's less risk in being a follower. You've got to accept that, acknowledge that, and play it for all it's worth in your marketing efforts. Set yourself up as a leader. **Give people in your marketplace a reason to consider you worthy of following.** Don't be shy; tell them exactly where they need to follow you and what you'll give them if they do. If you do a good, solid job, you'll find that people will flock to you. **Be the expert they're looking for... even if they won't admit it to themselves.**

There's a little joke that goes, "So many people think of themselves as leaders, but nobody's following them!" They're running around with this idea that they're leaders, but they're not influencing anybody or making anything happen. They're just leaders in their own mind... and really, who *wouldn't* want to be a leader? We admire our leaders. We want to be strong; we want to be confident; we want people to listen to us and to follow us. **And yet, if everybody *was* a leader, all moving in their individual directions, we'd have nothing but anarchy... and no one wants that.** Things are chaotic enough as it is.

So while most people want to think that they're leaders, in their secret hearts, they're really followers—and that's all they want to be. They want someone to believe in, someone to trust, someone to do most of the thinking and heavy lifting for them for them: experts who have gone where they want to go, and who can lead them safely on the path they want to be on. **People want certainty more than anything else, and so they'll take shortcuts toward that certainty by giving experts their money to lead them and safeguard their interests.**

Set yourself up as a credible expert, projecting yourself as a person with the answers, so people can take a shortcut toward safety. In so doing, they know that if all goes right—if you really are what you say you are, and you can do what you say you're going to—then ultimately they're going to get where they want to go even faster. **And to accomplish this, you need to really put yourself out there!** It amazes me that, even in this day and age, most marketers don't build strong personalities within their promotional materials. They're not really putting themselves on the line. Look: people want to do business with other *people*. But they have to be people who have the answers, who've gone where the prospect wants to go, who have a strong, credible reason for wanting to help the prospect. **Most of all, the leader has to be filled with confidence and enthusiasm.**

There was a group back in the 1970s called "EST," and it was huge. They had hundreds of thousands of followers who paid big bucks to be part of the group, and so they made millions of dollars. The founder was once quoted as saying, "Most people are running around with their umbilical cords, looking for someplace to plug in." He hit the nail on the head. That's exactly what he gave his followers when he created the EST movement—which the government ultimately shut down. It's an interesting story, if you ever want to Google it.

The point is, let people follow you. Give them a reason to do so... and watch the money come pouring in!

CHAPTER SEVEN

You serve yourself best — *when you serve others the most.*

You Serve Yourself Best When You Serve Others the Most

You serve yourself best when you serve others the most.

To some people, this statement sounds like a New Age, pop-culture mantra—a cute saying you'd find in a $12.95 success book. It definitely doesn't sound like a very profound secret; in fact, it doesn't sound like a secret at all. The sentiment ought to be self-obvious. **But so many businesspeople ignore this. They try to serve themselves first, and don't give a damn about anyone else.** Some of the smartest people on the planet aren't making the kind of money that they could and should be making because of such behavior. They struggle financially all their lives, barely making it, because they never learned this simple secret; and if they did, they ignored the lesson.

They're highly egotistical people, you see. You can say that about many successful individuals, but despite their intelligence and talent, most of these people are failures because they're total jerks to be around and nobody wants to do business with them. Instead of attracting people, which is crucial, all they do is repel them.

And then there are the others who, whenever you try to do business with them or have any relationship with them at all, just want to suck you dry. They're needy, and they're always coming at you so hard that it grates on you after a while. They're not thinking about you; they're not trying to look out for you, and they're not trying to serve you in any way. It's all about them—what are you going to do for them, and how soon can you do it? After a while, you just try to avoid them at all costs.

From personal experience, I can tell you that the real avenue to success is to develop deep, mutually beneficial relationships with everyone you work with. When you try to look out for people, they'll do the same for you—and you'll profit in a number of ways. Now, although the idea of serving yourself best when you serve others the most sounds like common sense, it's less common than it should be in today's business world. Some people call it "old school," as if there's something wrong with that. **And yet, it's the tried and true method for getting rich.** I won't insult your intelligence by telling you that it's easy to get rich, because sometimes it's very hard indeed. **But it becomes infinitely easier when you work with and surround yourself with the right people.**

We teach a four-step strategy for getting rich called "The Four Cornerstones of Wealth." Those cornerstones are straightforward enough, resulting in a simple equation: **You have to get involved in the right opportunities, at the right time, with the right people, with the right plan or implementation. Having good people is the golden key supporting all four of those cornerstones.** You find the right opportunities at the right time by being involved with the right people. You develop the right implementation by being involved with the right people—people who can help you, people who can take you from where you are now to wherever you want to go. Surround yourselves with the best and the brightest people, those who are also trustworthy and dependable—people you can count on. **When you find people like that, don't let them go.** In fact, try to create situations where they'll stay, where they'll continue to work with or for you for as long as possible—because those people make you money. **They'll** *always* **make you money. It's always been like that; it'll always be like that.**

You have to create win/win situations in order for this to occur. You have to help others get what they want, and create the right environments that make it good for them, so they'll help you get what *you* want.

One of the misconceptions that so many people have is that the individuals at the top of the business game, those who are doing the best and making the most money, are all a bunch of greedy S.O.B.s who are only looking out for themselves. The idea is that they're out to screw everybody, and it's always win/lose; that is, they win by causing you to lose. And yes, there *are* people like that, and because it's a very small world and bad news travels so fast, you're likely to hear about them more quickly than you hear about the good majority.

One of the smartest marketers I know—a man who's right up there at the very top of many lists of successful marketers—has a general rule which I really like and that I'm thinking about adopting. **When somebody approaches him about doing a joint venture, he always asks them for three references from other people they've done successful JV deals with.** If they can't give come up with those references, he says, "Well, when you do get those, come back and see me." He doesn't want to be a guinea pig; he's only looking for people with a history of good performance. If they can't provide glowing, positive references, he doesn't want to take a chance with them.

Business is a small world, and the higher you go, the smaller it seems. People in this business like to share contacts, sources, and joint venture partners—and they do talk. When somebody is a good person, you'll hear about it; but you'll especially hear about the bad people, because people like to warn each other about the bad more than they like to talk about the good. **Your reputation will precede you, so you definitely want to do all you can to create those situations where people *like* working with you, and prefer to hang around.** So you really do serve yourself best when you serve others the most. Simply put, treating people well makes you money.

In the long term, you're never going to attract the right kind of people in your life by screwing people around, or by taking advantage of them, or by using them, or by manipulating them to their detriment. **You attract the right people in your life by building a reputation for treating people *right*.** The most successful people in business learn this principal early and apply it forever after.

Here's an example of this in action. Our company is developing a giant Internet portal for the alternative health market—something similar to WebMD, but for unconventional medicine. It's a massive project. Chris Lakey, our Director of Marketing, is in charge of it—and I say without fear of contradiction that without Chris, there is no way on God's green Earth that it would ever work. **He's central to this whole thing. And he, himself, has relationships that go back a decade with**

the company in Malaysia that's helping us with this. There's a positive relationship with our global partner that has instilled in him a high level of trust. These are people that he can go to whenever he's confused or needs help with a particular aspect of the project.

This is a huge company that's already paid out almost _two billion dollars_ just in the last 10 years alone to the kind of people we're now working with through our portal. We have affiliated ourselves with them, and we trust in them because Chris has a relationship with these people that goes back for a decade. They know him. He can get through to the people at the top. Whenever he has a problem, he knows exactly who to call—and they take his call. That's what happens when you build win/win relationships. **That's the whole basis of this "secret": You just create win/win situations where everyone makes money.**

My relationship with Chris himself goes back 20 years now. We have similar deep, long-term relationships with a number of our other staff members, many of whom are also involved in this project. **You develop an almost telepathic level of communication when you've been involved in solid, positive relationships with people for years; and we believe that will ultimately make this project phenomenally successful.** Our goal is to do $100 million worth of business a year, and we firmly believe that we can do that. **Part of the reason we believe this is because we're leveraging all these established relationships, and making sure everyone wins.** If you're looking for a way to make easy money, this is it!

Here's another example. We've got a joint venture partner

we did a deal with last year who recently called us up and told us he had something red hot. Because we trusted him and expected we'd make big money off this project, we kept pressing him for specific details. He didn't want to give us any, because he was just figuring it out himself; but because we had a deep trust in him and had been working closely with him for about seven years, we gave him our endorsement... even though we really didn't know anything about the project. **There's no way we would have done anything like that without that prior relationship in place.**

But because the trust was there, because he liked working with us and we liked working with him (which is central to this idea), we said, "Sure, go ahead!" **We basically gave him carte blanche access to some of our best clients... and before long, over $100,000 came pouring into our coffers.** We didn't even know anything about this deal, and he was just getting started himself... but it was superbly profitable. Again, it's all about working with the right people with the right timing, with the right implementation, and the right opportunities.

We have another deal that's instrumental to us being involved on the Internet. We have a long history with electronic marketing; soon we'll be celebrating our 20th year at it. As I've mentioned in earlier, by the early 1990s we were involved with Computer Bulletin Boards through one of the brilliant joint venture partners we were working with back then. Then, when the Internet came along and gave us access to billions of people, he was right there with us. **He made us a ton of money—but we made him a ton of money, too. We were looking out for him and he was looking out for us.** We had certain things that we brought to the table when it came to marketing, advertising, and promotions; and he had certain things that he brought to the table when it came to actual Web development and the specific know-how that we needed but lacked. We made millions and millions of dollars together.

Another quick story: Russ von Hoelscher initially got us involved in seminars, and we had our first on September 22, 1990. We were scared to death at the time; my wife Eileen and I wouldn't even get up on the stage and speak, we were so frightened. We did talk to people later, in the back of the room and in the hallways. Russ, our joint venture partner, put it all together for us and made that happen. The seminar business is an integral part of our company now, something that we value and cherish a great deal... and we have Russ to thank for that. **He was looking out for us, and over the years, we've tried to do everything possible to look out for him.**

Where would our company be without these people? Nowhere. Thanks to these individuals and the relationships we've developed with them, and all of their ideas that we've adopted and adapted, we've been going strong for over 20 years. And yes, they've learned and earned a lot from us along the way too. It's been win/win all the way!

We've got a brand new relationship that we hope will develop into a similar win/win scenario. **We're getting involved in a whole new marketplace now—a much bigger marketplace than the one we're currently in.** But the reason we were able to find this certain person we're working with now was because we knew the right contacts to begin with, based on a prior relationship that goes back 20 years. This person we knew back then is now in this giant market; and he wouldn't even have taken our phone call had we not known him and worked with him 20 years ago.

But we *did* get through to him, because he remembered us fondly; and **he then gave us access to this source who only works with select individuals and companies, and she is top-notch, and she's going to make us a ton of money.** We're also going to make *her* a ton of money. When I told her we would do an exclusive deal with her and her alone, she lit up; she appreciated that. That made her happy and excited because that's what she's looking for, too. So again, it's a win/win situation. You serve yourself best by serving others the most.

Think about it: that's a kind of Golden Rule, isn't it? Zig Ziglar has a similar quote, where he says you can get everything you want by helping other people get what *they* want. Some people call this "enlightened capitalism," or "enlightened selfishness," as I've mentioned in a previously. **All it boils down to is serving other people so you can obtain a benefit yourself.** It's not altruism, though it's true that if you do good things, good things will come to you.

That's basically the foundation of our company, and has been from the very beginning. Back in 1988, when Eileen and I found something that worked to make money for us, **we quickly decided to make a business out of sharing that success.** Many other companies were started in similar fashion for similar reasons, so this is hardly a new idea... and yet I think a lot of people just forget about things like this. **The simplicity, perhaps, allows it to be overlooked.** But it's an important point to rediscover—if not to discover for the first time.

Now, there are a couple of different aspects to consider here. First, there's the service to your marketplace or clientele; and then there's the service you provide to your suppliers and the other people you work with to get your product to market (or whatever you do to serve your customers). **You have to have both of those sets of relationships working at the same time in order to best serve yourself and others.**

Speaking of developing good relationships with suppliers: our relationship with our printer is a great example. It goes back a long way, and we're constantly doing whatever we can to help each other make money. It's probably a 45-minute trip from his print shop to our door, and yet he makes that trip almost on a daily basis. If we told him we needed something, he would be here. He's made two trips in one day before, in fact. **So he serves us, and we serve him.** We give him lots of printing business, which allows us to serve our customers in turn, because some of the material he prints ends up in our customers' hands. **It works like a triangle, really, where we're all helping and serving each other.** That's how *our* business model works, in any case; other businesses may handle their relationships differently.

That said, this idea of serving others to serve yourself is, I think, a foundational principle of small businesses of all kinds. Sometimes, when you have too large a company, the ability to serve people (especially within your company) gets lost. Often, a large company ends up getting bogged down in bureaucracy, or they're so large they can gain influence in political ways that allow them to dominate a market or create a monopoly, or engage in other activities where they're not really serving the marketplace anymore. At that point, they're just doing what they can to make as much money as possible. So this is really a small business principle at heart. It's much easier for a small business to serve people—but that doesn't mean that you need to give up this principle if your company does become large.

The fact is, offering incredible customer service is one of the ways that you can actually compete against large companies that seem to have an unfair advantage. The found of Wal-Mart, Sam Walton himself, pointed this out in his book *Made in America.* Too often, small businesses just give up when Wal-Mart or similar chains come to town; but that's a mistake. As Walton puts it, all he can offer is convenience and low price; customer service is there, but it's not really part of the equation in such a huge, impersonal place. **Well, small businesses can excel at customer service.** They don't need to run and hide in the face of stiff competition—and they shouldn't!

There was a nice little movie starring Tom Hanks and Meg Ryan a while back called *You've Got Mail* that explored this theme. Meg Ryan owns a little bookstore, and Tom Hanks is one of the executives of a huge chain called Fox Books, something like Barnes & Noble. Well, they put a big Fox Bookstore right around the corner from Meg Ryan's store, and eventually the little bookstore has to go out of business. Whenever I watch that movie, I think about the fact that the little bookstore offered so much that that giant chain couldn't; and, hopefully (in my mind anyway), the reason they went under was because they weren't doing a good job of marketing the fact that they were better at serving their customers than the Fox bookstore.

CHAPTER SEVEN: You Serve Yourself Best When You Serve Others the Most

Think of that movie as just an example of the difference between what a big business can offer for its customers—which might be nothing more than selection and low prices—versus what a small business can offer in the terms of personal service, and other things that a big box store could never (or simply would never) do for you. **If you own a small business, you can at least feel confident that you have the potential to do a lot more for people, and serve your marketplace, much better than a big company can or would care to.** And there are ways and ways of doing this, as the old saying goes.

Centuries ago, a man named Adam Smith wrote a book called *An Inquiry Into the Nature and Causes of the Wealth of Nations*. **One of the principles in that book was the division of labor, and it comes to mind whenever I think about this principle of serving other people. Smith uses it as a point about productivity, but I think it has parallels here and can be applied to small businesses in your efforts to serve your customers to the maximum extent possible.** He uses a pen factory to talk about the need for specialization, in terms of maximizing productivity (which again, at its most basic level, is about serving your customers in the best possible way). If a person were to have to make all the parts of a pen and then put them together, they could produce only so many pens in a day. But if you break that labor down into several different parts, so that one person makes this piece of the pen, another person makes another, and someone else puts them all together; well, each person can get very good at doing their one part, and you can increase overall production.

He also uses the example of a common blacksmith, so you

can see how old his book is. In any case, a common smith, though accustomed to handling a hammer, might never have been asked to make nails. While he might eventually be able to figure out how to do so, it might take him a while. But Smith points out that he'd seen "several boys under 20 years of age who had never used any other trade except making nails, and when they were exerting themselves they could make, each of them, up to 2,300 nails a day." **His point is that a division of labor can, ultimately, increase overall productivity.**

How does this apply to service? **Small businesses need to be agile in order to succeed, their owners thoughtful about how they can best serve the people who serve them.** So many never even take the time to think about how they can break down their processes and rebuild them to maximize productivity (i.e., service). **Consider outsourcing, which is hiring specialists outside the company to do things they can do better and more cheaply than you.** Serve them by hiring them, and let them serve you by maximizing your productivity, so you can maximize your service to your customers. Simple enough.

Consider our printer, whom I mentioned earlier. We have an excellent relationship with him. He serves us and we serve him, by providing jobs for him to do; and so he keeps his employees working and his business stays open. That's not our primary responsibility, but it *is* a result of us using him and the services he provides. I also spoke earlier of the company in Malaysia, and our worldwide partner. Those companies provide valuable services to us, so they're serving us. We're using them—and therefore, serving them by providing them with income—and as a result, our customers get better served because we're able to do more for them. **Clearly, the outsourcing idea works up and down the business scale at all levels; we're able to serve our customers because we're relying on the services of other companies, other entities that are doing work for us. It all works together.**

For me, that's the connection between this principle of service and Adam Smith's concept of the division of labor. **Too often, small business owners try to do everything themselves.** They act as the point of sale to the customer, so they're being the cashier. They're probably doing all the books, filing their own taxes, and handling all the paperwork. They're the ones going to the store and buying the supplies. They're wearing all those hats all at the same time.

It's better to divide up that labor. **Why do something worth maybe $10 an hour when you can make $100 if you focus on the important things?** Hire someone for $10 to do that work, and reap an extra $90. It's worth it. Yes, you could do it yourself, but so what? By dividing up the labor, you can actually increase productivity, make more money—and more effectively serve your customers. In the end you serve yourself best, you make your company more productive, by serving other people more. So let other people do more things for you.

If you can serve your customers better, they'll naturally be happier. They'll do more business with you, so your company will make more profit. You can farm out more work to your outsourcers, you'll need to buy more supplies, and your employees have plenty to do. Everybody's happy all around. Everybody wins under the service model, because in the end, everyone's better off—and there's nothing wrong with that. I don't think it's selfish thing to want to better yourself; that's probably why you're in business in the first place. **Your business is there to not only serve other people, but to serve you as well.** Unless you've started a charity, you're there to earn money and provide for your family. Don't feel bad about that!

It's easy for this idea of "enlightened selfishness" to get twisted the wrong way, or for the service model to simply get abandoned altogether; that's obvious, since so many people are failing to do what I've discussed here. But don't just give the concept of service; it's far from outdated, especially in the small business arena. **Think hard about how you can serve your customers to the utmost—because when you do that, you're just serving yourself, too.**

CHAPTER EIGHT

Your marketing (everything you do to get more customers and keep them spending more money for life) is only limited by your imagination.

Remember that every time you are going through a sales slump or a cash-flow crisis.

Your Marketing is Only Limited by Your Imagination

As I've pointed out before, marketing is everything that you do to attract and keep customers. **If you want to make more money, then you need to sell more stuff to more people, more often, for more profits per transaction, with greater efficiency.** That's it in a nutshell—and ultimately, how you accomplish that is limited only by your imagination. Whether that's the good news or bad news is up to you to decide and take action on. Remember that when you go through a sales slump or cash flow crisis. If you're wondering who to blame, go to the nearest mirror and point your finger at the person you see reflected there. **If you can't think of something that can boost sales, then consider finding someone else to work with who can.**

We're getting involved with a whole new marketplace right now, one that's much bigger than the market we've been in for the last 23 years. We're working with some top-notch people, and they understand this market in a very deep way. They can acquire for us the very best of all the available mailing lists—the ones that other companies are using to make a nice profit. And yet, still we have to test like crazy before we know how our ideas are going to be received, and what's going to work to make us a profit. **We've got to try a lot of different ideas, including some novel foundational principles that we're building our new company on. It requires a huge amount of creativity.**

TOTAL SUCCESS!

In a situation like this one, it's crucial that you strive to know your customers at the most intimate level possible. Each time you test something new, you're finding out what people really want. **What you're doing is basically paying for that information.** Then you take elements of the very best results, and incorporate those elements into the next test, while testing new things as well. **In so doing, you continue to find newer and better ways to develop the kinds of promotions that excite your clientele and prospects the most.** You continue to solidify your unique selling position—those things that separate you from everybody else—in the marketplace. Ideally, you get better as you go along. **At the same time, you're constantly looking for what's new and what's next.** What do people want the most today—especially, what do people want the most that they're not getting? What are some of the biggest problems in the marketplace? How can you fix them?

Right now, we're putting together a promotion that uses a principle we discovered by accident 15 years ago. Back then, we were working with a website developer—and we had a huge production problem. The customer demand for our websites was incredibly high, because the World Wide Web was still brand new; **but it took us *forever* to get those websites tested, and it was slowing the whole process down.** We knew that if we could speed up the testing process, we could double, triple, even quadruple our sales.

Our solution was to create a special Beta Tester Offer. We made our customers a deal that nobody else got. It was an incredible bargain for them, providing them with a big bundle of websites at a phenomenally reduced price if they would help us with the testing process. Now, we were just looking at it as a way for us to develop more websites faster; and yet, what we found was that people went crazy over this idea. **They loved the fact that we were giving them a great price for a good reason... because people are often very suspicious when you offer them something for a low price.** They're especially suspicious if they can't see any strings attached. But we were still making a profit as we gave our customers this tremendous bargain, and they loved it and trusted it because they saw that it was credible.

You see, while people love bargains, they hate cheap stuff. **What they want is expensive stuff for dirt-cheap prices... and that's exactly what we were giving them.** It was a true, good reason to have a sale. The websites needed to be tested, and by letting them help us with the testing, we were able to get these websites onto the market a lot faster. Since it was all on the up-and-up, customers snapped up our offer, **we started developing more and more websites faster, and what did we do then? We had more Beta Tester promotions!**

This type of promotion has *never* failed to make us a significant profit. Some of the iterations have produced profits of hundreds of thousands of dollars; some have produced profits amounting to millions of dollars... but in all cases, they've been sure-fire promotions that we can count on to profit us. And we would never have come up with the Beta Tester idea had we not been committed to trying out and testing all kinds of things, and paying close attention to the results. **When you find something that really works, you need to figure out as many ways as you can to roll it out. That's essentially what we've done with these Beta Tester offers... and we've been doing it profitably**

TOTAL SUCCESS!

for 15 years.

And here's the shocking thing: to the best of my knowledge, we're the only company doing this. We've had some of the same competitors now for many years, and they're seeded on all the Direct Mail lists we use. Every time we do a promotion of this type, it goes out to them. The fact that nobody has taken advantage of this and simply copied our offer is just mind-boggling to me. On the one hand, I'm excited by that; if others *were* copying us, this offer wouldn't continue to work as phenomenally well as it has. On the other hand, I have to scratch my head and wonder *why* they haven't copied us. **You see, when a promotion is repeated consistently, that's a sure indication that it's profitable, which makes it worth copying at some level.** And yet nobody has copied us at all on this Beta Tester concept.

There are two main lessons here. **First, you've got to be willing to test all kinds of different ideas.** We had no idea that this was going to be such a phenomenal hit for us before we tried it—that it would in fact work for us like magic, and prove to be a surefire hit that we could always count on. But we were open and receptive to trying all kinds of things, and that's how we stumbled upon this concept. To be honest, we initially just wanted to give our customers a special price if they would help us, too.

Lesson Two: Don't make the mistake that our competitors have. Study your competitors and consider modeling your offers on things that have worked for them. Get on their mailing lists, find out what's working the best for them, and find ways to incorporate those elements into your offers. Look for new ways to package your offers, and

112

brainstorm with what you've found on a regular basis.

Every morning at 5:00 or 5:30 in the morning, I get up and start looking for ideas. I do this seven days a week, and I've done it for many years now; I've trained my brain to start thinking about ways to increase sales every morning. Some days, no ideas come to me at all; on other days, the ideas flow like water from a busted fire hydrant, and I can't shut them off. I just want to get on the phone with Chris Lakey and other bright people and throw ideas back and forth, because I'm so pumped about it all.

This is another good lesson for you. **Brainstorm at a set time every day.** If you're an early morning person like I am, it's a perfect way to start your day. If your mind works best at one in the morning, when the rest of the family is asleep, then do it at that time. In any case, train yourself to do it at the same time every day, so your subconscious mind knows that this is the time to come up with creative work. And by the way, it *is* work. Don't let anybody fool you about that. Sure, some of it's a lot of fun, but exercising your imagination takes real effort. **Fortunately, while you *are* limited only by your imagination, your imagination is like anything else: it's strengthened with use.** So if you don't have a lot of creative ideas at first, that just means you have to tone up your imagination. Flabby imagination muscles aren't very profitable.

So brainstorm with yourself, and then brainstorm with other people. I just can't express to you how many wonderful ideas come out of the lengthy conversations that Chris Lakey and I have many mornings. As often as three mornings out of every week, Chris and I will get on the phone for an hour or two—or sometimes even three hours. We have actually been known to speak on the phone, brainstorming ideas, for as long as four to five hours a day. We're bouncing ideas back and forth; he'll give me a spark of an idea and I'll run with it, or vice versa. Actually, we do this with all our staff, especially a group I call the "Core Four." That's Chris, me, our General Manager, Shelly Webster, and our Sales Manager, Drew Hansen.

During our brainstorm sessions, we're always asking ourselves and each other, "What's new? What's next? What could we do to inflame our prospect's desires? What can we do to create those great, irresistible offers the customers just can't say no to? What offers will get them to stand in line with money in hand, and practically beg us to take that money?" Those are the kinds of things that we're looking for on a regular basis... and in business, you find what you look for. The more you look for these things, the more you'll find them.

Marketing requires a great deal of brain exercise, and a willingness to pursue creativity. Think back to when you were a child. We're all very creative early in life, but as we mature, we lose some of that creativity. In the end, some of us don't end up thinking much at all... and unfortunately, the result is that many entrepreneurs are basically walking zombies. We don't exercise our brains in the things that matter. Many of us don't read much anymore, so we're losing out on that form of knowledge and communication. We may watch some TV, but we're not watching informative TV. It's no wonder that a lot of people struggle in business in the creativity department. You have to exercise your brain and keep those creative juices flowing.

We see a lot of creativity in kids: they draw a lot, they play pretend, and they tell wild, interesting stories. At some point, though, we start being molded in the ways that society expects, and we get pushed through an education system that dumbs us down and makes us all uniform. We lose that creativity. Even writing styles are regulated. Chris Lakey has six kids ranging in age from a freshman in high school down to a preschooler, and he's noticed that among the oldest kids, the writing assignments are very specific regarding how they have to write: the style, the words they use... even the number of paragraphs, sometimes. It's all very uniform, with specific standards and formats. If they don't do it the way the teacher says they're supposed to, then they get counted off for that.

That just one example of the way you gradually lose your creativity and imagination as you mature, and have to conform to what's expected of you. It flows in all kinds of ways as we move from childhood to adulthood. **By the time you're an adult, the creative process has been stifled enough that you pretty much just do what people expect you to do.** The media, the government, the public at large—they all have expectations for you. If you don't behave like they want you to, you're considered an outcast, an outsider; there's something wrong with you.

This flows right over into business. Now, if you're just an average Joe working for somebody else, doing what they want you to do anyway, that's usually not a problem. You can float through life, be a conformist, and never cause any trouble. You can live a boring, mediocre life, and do just fine. But if you're trying to run a small business, that kind of thinking will cause you to fail. You have to fight the urge to be normal when it comes to business; you have to be creative. **The success of**

your marketing—all the things you do to bring in new customers, or to do more business with your existing customers—hinges on your ability to use your imagination to exercise those creative juices and stir up business for yourself. Among other things, that means running wild promotions to attract new customers.

This is especially true for small retail businesses. If you're not doing anything to separate yourself, to create a unique space for yourself in your marketplace, you're probably going to be viewed as just another little shop—like every other business in that field. There's nothing to separate you from your competitors; there's no reason your customers should shop at your store or eat at your restaurant instead of at your competitors'. On the other hand, **what if you could make yourself stand out somehow, so that you're the obvious first choice?**

Think about the wild, crazy businesses in your town. Most towns have a few. They're the ones who do the weird ads on TV, and who do the strange things in the newspaper, or you see them out there advertising with costumed mascots, or they mail you odd-looking brochures and flyers. In other words, they do things to capture your imagination and get your business. All those things are dreamed up by some marketer exercising their creativity to sell their products and services, or at least to get you in their door. If you're a small business owner, you have to take a page from their playbook. **Turn on the creativity; get those juices flowing. Absolutely resist the urge to be average, to just maintain the status quo; instead, do your best to stand out in the marketplace.**

Remember this principle every time you're going through a

slump or a cash flow crisis. Any time you struggle to bring in sales and generate revenue, remember that creative marketing will solve most of those problems. There may be a few exceptions, but usually all you need to jazz up sluggish sales is a creative marketing campaign—something to shake up the marketplace, to grab people's attention so they're looking at you instead of at your competitors. **Ultimately, the success or failure of your marketing depends largely on your ability not to be boring.** Customers always want to be wowed—and so you need to wow them and wake them up.

Your customers are looking for things that are new and exciting. If there's nothing new or exciting to be had, then it's up to you to create something that is.

Remember how I've emphasized the importance of testing? That's one way to determine what works with your marketplace. We've got a promotion right now where, at the beginning, we tested two different versions. One version had a slightly different hook than the other; when we do a test like this, we call it an "A-B Split Test." **Well, one of the versions bombed: it made no money at all. The other, in which we came up with a crazy new hook, performed phenomenally well—and now we're rolling out with that version.** We might never have tapped that profitable alternative had we not tested that new hook.

If you want average results, be average. If you want above-average results, be above average. It's as simple as that. **You've got to be willing to stick your neck out a little; be outrageous, try different things, be wild and crazy—and take big risks.** I'm talking about things that scare you a little, where you make a lot of promises to your prospects and then think, "Oh, my God, are we really going to be able to do these things?" If you're a little scared, a little nervous, then you're doing it right. If you're not, you're not taking a big enough risk.

Do things that push the envelope in an attempt to cause your customers to wake up and ask, "What *is* this?" Snap them out of their standard boredom with what we call "marketing incest"—where everybody is just copying everybody else, and it's all gone flat and boring. Common, everyday marketing doesn't stand out or separate you from everybody else. It doesn't wake people up; it doesn't get their attention; it doesn't excite them; it doesn't make them enthusiastic.

So how do you accomplish this? The best thing you can possibly do is study what other people are doing, and just rule out the same old, same old. **When you see somebody doing something else that's innovative and different, make note of it and try to analyze it.** While a lot of marketing success is emotion-based, it *does* leave clues. When you find something that other people are doing that's different and unique and really works, that can lead you to a kissing cousin of the same idea. **You shouldn't precisely copy what they're doing, but you can definitely learn from observing.**

So pay attention. Get on the other side of the cash register. **Start looking at your competitors' marketing not from a consumer's point of view, but from a fellow marketer's point of view.** Start learning how to create irresistible offers that help other people get the competitive advantages they seek, so you can get the competitive advantage *you* seek.

CHAPTER NINE

**Keep feeding the fire of your enthusiasm —
so it <u>always</u> burns brightly!**

- ✓ Get involved in exciting new projects that stir your blood!

- ✓ Stay excited about the future!

- ✓ Set bigger goals and grander visions!

- ✓ "If you want to turn your hours into minutes, renew your enthusiasm!"
  Papyrus

Keep Feeding the Fire of Your Enthusiasm

Keep feeding the fire of your enthusiasm, so that it always burns brightly. Get involved in exciting new projects that stir your blood. Stay excited about the future. **Set bigger goals and grander visions.** "If you want to turn your hours into minutes, renew your enthusiasm." That last is a quote from Papyrus, someone who lived many thousands of years ago.

Look, I don't know about you, but for me, part of the joy of life is when my hours *do* turn into minutes—when I'm doing something that I'm so involved in that all of a sudden I look up at the clock, and a couple of hours have gone by. That's a great thing for me. **It's all about setting huge goals, taking huge risks, doing things that excite you, even doing things that scare you a little.** Somebody once told me that if a new idea doesn't scare you, you shouldn't do it. It's got to be big, it's got to be bold!

There's another quote by David Burnham, an architect who died a century ago, that goes, "Make no little plans. They have no magic to stir men's blood." And that's what we have to do as marketers: stir people's blood. In order to get them to give us their money, we have to get them fired up and excited first. We have to produce offers that are big, bold, and audacious, that provide tremendous value, and especially that are new and exciting! **Bored people don't buy, and bored customers don't** *re*-**buy.** If you keep trying to sell the same old stuff to your customers repeatedly, if you're not trying to do things to serve it up bigger and better every time, your customers will go elsewhere. **People want do business with other people and companies who are going someplace exciting.**

If you're reading this, you want to get rich—whatever that means to you. In any case, you want to make a lot of money. Well, the only legal, ethical, and moral way to do that is to create offers that are so irresistible that people just cannot contain themselves, to the point where they gladly exchange their money for what you're offering. Then you need to keep building up your established business relationships, so that they'll re-buy from you again and again for years. **That's the overall secret of profitability that all super-successful companies have in common.**

To stir the blood, your offer has to be big, bold, and enthusiastic. **It's got to excite *you*, so you can transmit that excitement to your customers.** The more excited you are, the more excited your prospective buyers and existing customers will be.

Most businesspeople prefer to play it far too conservatively. I know people right now who are struggling financially because they're still trying to re-sell the same tired, worn-out stuff that, quite frankly, isn't very exciting to people anymore. **The market does change, in the sense that it always demands something new and exciting.** People who are not tapping into this reality are not getting their fair share of the marketplace. Nobody wants their old crap anymore... and so they fail. And it's their own fault.

Look around at all your competitors, especially the ones who are doing the very best, and take notes on what they're doing. Simultaneously, **study your prospects and determine what they want the most in terms of benefits.** Think deeply about all this, and then ask yourself, "What can I do to create the biggest, boldest, most exciting, most valuable offers possible? What can I do to prove to my prospects that the money I'm asking in return is of relatively little value, compared to what I'm offering?"

If you can provide something that's new and exciting *and* offers the potential long-term benefits that your buyers are looking for, then the question is not, "Will I get rich?" The question becomes, "How rich will I get, and how long will it take for me to get there?" Because I promise you, **if you'll follow that simple formula, all the money you want and need is going to come to you.** That money is out there right now, in people's bank accounts and credit cards; you just have to formulate an effective way to tap it.

This is a very important point, one that took me a while to grasp. The same is true of many people who want to get rich: **they don't understand, at a deep level, that the money *is* out there, and that they have to find a way to get people to legitimately want to give it to them.** Back when I was getting started 30 years ago, if someone had asked, "How are you going to make your millions?", I wouldn't have been able to answer them.

But the money *is* there, in quantities that stagger the imagination, among those millions of people who are searching for the specific benefits that *you* can give them. **Right now, we**

have an offer that perfectly illustrates this. It's big, bold, fresh, new, and exciting... and it's a little scary for us. Our new project is called our "Health Resource Portal," and it's got us living on the edge here at M.O.R.E., Inc. We've been working for a long time on this, and it was a grand plan to start with.

Basically, the Health Resource Portal is an alternative health web portal connecting to over 2,000 moneymaking websites—2,000 ways to get paid instant cash from the automatic sale of health-related products or services to a worldwide marketplace of tens of millions of people, in 145 different nations all around the world. **We're in the process of developing a $100 million-a-year business plan that outlines our goal of bringing in that much money or more. In fact, we've got plans to bring in over one billion dollars in our first 15 years alone.**

We've built all of this around a huge gap in a trillion-dollar-a year industry that's fairly hidden—in fact, it's known to only a small group of people. Most of the people who do know about it are getting very, very wealthy; a small group of companies is making hundreds of millions a year at it, and an even smaller group is making *billions* of dollars a year in sales. **This derives from the simple fact that they truly understand how to fill this gap.**

Essentially, this offer gives millions of people the things they want the most: better health and more wealth. In fact, I'm working on a book right now with that very same title: *How to Get Better Health and More Wealth.* We're offering people 2,000 of our powerful moneymaking websites, valued at $98.79 each—a real world value of $197,580. Of course, we're not

124

charging them that much. The point is, everything about this offer reeks of the BIG and BOLD. It's exciting, new, and fresh—and it's different!

Again, it's got us living on the edge right now. It's feeding the fire of our enthusiasm—and doing the same for those of our customers who are already involved with us. Everything about this offer is big and bold, including the fact that for a small group of people, we have a special bonus that promises them a percentage of every dollar that we ever bring in… no matter how big we get. And I think we'll get quite big, because there are tens of millions of people in those 145 nations who are potential buyers from all 2,000 of our websites. The commonality that these people have is that many are getting older, and as you may know, once you're exceeded age 40, your body basically starts falling apart.

The older you get, the more aware you are of the fact that you're more susceptible to diseases and you need more energy, more vitality. You want to lose weight, because the fat starts accumulating; and basically, your body starts to "rust out" a little, and you've got to take better care of yourself. **So people are looking for better health. They want to live longer, they want to feel better, they want to lose weight, they want more energy and more vitality, and they don't want to die of all of the deadly diseases that are killing so many other people before their time.**

Then there's the wealth angle. Millions of people are looking for a way to make more money, and they'd jump at the chance if they just had a way to do it without all the pain, problems, headaches, and hassles that you get with a traditional business. **By marrying wealth and health together, we're creating something that we firmly believe is going to generate many tens of millions of dollars in revenue for us and our investors.** That is, of course, if we're right in our assumptions; and admittedly, they're only educated guesses, because nobody knows the future. So we're not making any specific promises to our clients, only the promise of potential profits. But if we're right, the people who get involved with us are going to become financially set for life. **This is something that's going to change their lives—and it's big and exciting.** It's also a little scary for us, because we're moving into a brand new area that's tremendously bigger than what we've done now for the past 23 years.

But that's what life is all about. It's what *business* is all about. **If you want a thriving business, if you want to be a leader in your marketplace, you've got to look for and leverage big, exciting offers like the one we're creating.** You've got to put your energy into something that will stir people's blood—and something that will stir *your* blood, too. The more excited you are, the more you're going to transfer that excitement to the people you're trying to attract as customers.

Fueling your enthusiasm like this is one certain way to make sure that you avoid succumbing to mediocrity. Because, you see, it's the easiest thing in the world to just keep doing whatever it is you're doing right now; it takes effort to shift your inertia and change your direction, so most people don't bother to do so once they're set on a specific path. Well, that's the path to complacency; and you're likely to end up looking back on your life and wondering how you got where you are... and why the important things got bypassed along the way. **When you end up doing the same things over and over, you never experience the new... and you never have the chance to find something that works better than what you've always done.**

If you want to do something different, and want to get involved in something bigger, then **you need to move out of your comfort zone toward new and exciting projects that stir your blood.** Don't allow yourself to get stale or complacent; you've got to keep feeding the fire of your enthusiasm so that it always burns brightly.

Why does that matter? For one thing, you're never bored. For another, some of your best and brightest ideas come from the white-hot forge of the imagination—from those times when you're the most excited about something. This doesn't have to be limited to business, of course; it applies to anything you're interested in, from hobbies to sports. In fact, let's look a bit closer at sports.

If you're good at a sport, and you want to master it at a semi-pro or pro level, you definitely want to maintain your enthusiasm about it. Otherwise, at some point you'll become bored with the routine—especially the things you need to do to hone the edge of your mastery, such as practice and pre-season exhibitions. You don't mind playing the games because you can get worked up and excited about them; but if you can't get worked up and excited about the preparations for the game, then maybe it's time to retire from that sport and do something else.

I think football great Brett Favre epitomizes this sort of

world-weary boredom. Toward the end of his career, he would sign with a team right before the season started, skipping the pre-season and most of the practice altogether. I suspect he did that partly because his body was worn down, and partly because he was tired of the routine. He just wanted to play the games... and maybe he deserved that at that point in his career. But the fact of the matter is, a lot of your success on the field is determined by your success in the gym or in practice, whether you're fed up or bored with that routine or not.

It's much the same way with business. **You have to maintain your enthusiasm all the time, even when you're not in the middle of something that gets you especially excited.** Fortune favors not just the bold, but also the prepared. You've got to work hard in order to succeed; and to be willing to do so, you've got to stay excited about what you're doing. **As you're working toward your ultimate goals, you've got to keep feeding that fire of enthusiasm so that it always burns brightly.**

Remember: "If you want to turn your hours into minutes, renew your enthusiasm." When you're consistently excited about a project, when things are going really well for you and you're having fun, time passes faster—even as you become more productive. You get lost in your work. You really do have days when time flies—*because* you're having fun. **If high enthusiasm and energy rule your emotions, then a day can fly by.** You can look back on that day, however long it may be, and it feels like you've barely worked at all—even when you've accomplished a mountain of things. We all know that time can be subjective; and we've all experienced the exact opposite, when time seems to move as slow as molasses, and fifteen minutes can seem like hours.

Time itself doesn't move any differently; only your perception of it does. A minute is always 60 seconds. **The apparent variance in the lengths of your days is based largely upon the amount of enthusiasm you're experiencing.** The more excited and enthusiastic you are for a project, the faster time moves. Think about the times when you've watched a bad movie or sat there reading a book you really didn't want to read; you lack enthusiasm, so time crawls, doesn't it? On the other hand, if you're watching an action-packed movie that drags you in and tweaks your imagination, at the end you wonder, "Where did the time go?" Time flies when your enthusiasm is at its peak. That happens in all kinds of experiences, and it certainly happens in business.

This is holding true for us with our Health Portal project. **We're entering the health market in a major way, and we're really excited about it. There's a lot of energy and enthusiasm crackling through this project—and yes, there's a lot of pressure.** There are plenty of unknown factors to deal with, and significant risks on a number of fronts. The easiest thing for us to do would be to sit back and keep doing what we've always done in the past, in order to get the results we've always gotten... and just let the status quo take over. That's sort of like being on an assembly line in a factory. The days go on, and you pretty much have the same experience every day, day after day.

But that can be boring, and if your enthusiasm slips, it can kill the business. **And the thing is, we've had a long-standing**

goal for several years now to enter this marketplace; it just happens that the timing is right to do it now. A number of factors came together, you see, and we felt like it was the right time to move—and so we jumped. As I'm writing this, we've just kicked off the project. We're still at the end of the beginning; it all starts here. **We've hit a high-pressure point, where a lot of complex things are coming together.** Deadlines are pressuring us, and we're working to bring everything at this beginning to a successful conclusion.

As we enter the second phase, we'll still be doing some testing, but the initial production phases will have been completed. Our enthusiasm for this project has been really high for many weeks now, and that's led to some highly productive periods—which means that the days have just flown by.

Early on, when it was a brand new idea, enthusiasm was high; but there were a lot of days between that point and where I knew we needed to be as we wrapped up the initial phase. As things stated kicking off, I was enthused and excited—but there was less pressure than later on. The deadlines seemed a little further out and, while my enthusiasm always remained high, there were days when things were out of my control, and time passed more slowly. So I worked on other projects when I couldn't do much directly related to the Health Portal.

As the deadline loomed and my enthusiasm really keyed up, time sped up. I would imagine that a professional football player preparing for the Super Bowl feels the same way. **Your blood's hopping, and you feel full of energy.** You've practiced and made all the preparations, you've been gearing up, and now it's all culminating in this one event that you've been working toward. That how it felt for us as we neared the launch of our Health Portal. **There's still a lot of work to be done, but the enthusiasm through this entire beginning phase has been extremely high;** and that's kept us excited as we've implemented the imaginative things that helped us launch our new company in this new direction we're going in. Now we've just got to keep that enthusiasm alive.

As I've said, we have a $100-million-a-year plan we're working toward. That's one of the things that has kept our excitement high throughout the planning and implementation stages, and it's keeping our excitement high as we move on. **If we hadn't begun this project by thinking BIG from the very beginning, the enthusiasm might not have risen to the fever pitch we're now enjoying—and we would certainly have done things differently.** But we knew that we were going to be launching 2,000 websites through this Health Portal, and that it would have to be a huge, bold project as a result, just to get off the ground. We wanted to do something bigger than we've ever seen done before, to go where no one had gone before; and that required a lot of enthusiasm to offset the pressure and difficulties we would inevitably experience.

We could have had it easier, if we'd been willing to do something smaller and simpler. But there's a saying that goes, "Go big or go home." In poker terms, we wanted this to be "all in." We wanted to put all the chips on the table, to make this as big as we possibly could. We wanted to create something bold and daring, that people would look at and be impressed by—not impressed because of our ability, or at the Portal as a monument to our egos, but because they could clearly see the enormity of the dedication and the work that went into making this thing as awesome as it could possibly be. **We wanted it to be clear that we put in all the energy, time, and resources required to make it work, because we dreamed of penetrating this big marketplace not just for our own benefit, but for the benefit of the clients who wanted to join us there.** We wanted to see how far we could take this game of business, growing it in an entirely new direction.

That's what it's all about to us—the game. We've been getting ready for this game, our Super Bowl if you will, for quite some time—and now we've made our big entrance. We've made a strong start, and now we're going to see how it works out as we show everyone why we're so excited about all this.

Phase One of the project is over; we're in the opening stages of Phase Two, which is perhaps just as challenging and difficult and has its own issues and, hopefully, its own rewards. All of that will come as we continue being enthusiastic and excited with the project. **Our enthusiasm remains high, our blood is stirred, and we're truly excited for the future. That drives us to the actions we're taking with this new marketplace.** We're working very hard to make this everything that we envision it to be; and all the excitement and enthusiasm we're bringing to this project will hopefully result in a better product in the end, one that keeps us going and eager to see what's next.

You know, I can't imagine working the kind of job where you do the same thing over and over again at a factory, or where you push a button all day, or where you do anything repetitively... even something like scooping ice cream. I would

132

imagine it's really difficult to maintain your enthusiasm in a job like that. Even if you happen to run a business, the repetition can be such that the risk of falling into the mundane is high. You have to fight the feeling that you're just going through the motions for no real benefit; therefore, you *have* to find ways to jazz things up. **Do whatever you can to feed the fire of your enthusiasm so that it always burns brightly. Get involved in or *stay* involved in exciting projects that stir your blood.** Get excited about new opportunities, and keep setting bigger goals and grander visions. If you want to turn hours into minutes, just renew that enthusiasm

Enthusiasm can help you roll back the years, and both look and feel younger. Recently, I was watching a football game on TV, and one of my favorite past stars was there on the sidelines, watching his former team play. I won't mention him by name, but he's been retired now for 10 or 12 years. And I thought to myself, *God, he looks so old!* Then his team went into overtime and actually won the game, and he was down on the sidelines, cheering and all excited and filled with enthusiasm… and I swear, he looked at least 10 or 15 years younger then— maybe 20 years younger.

Enthusiasm is the juice of life, and it can be worth more than gold. **You get some of your best marketing ideas when you're consistently enthusiastic, because when you're really excited about something, the ideas just flow to you.** I'm a copywriter, and in my experience, when I can turn that enthusiasm up to a fiery glow, it's almost like the words just flow out of me fully formed. It's like all I'm doing is dictating something already written, and sometimes, the words come through faster than I can type them. I'm constantly tripping up on my fingers, misspelling words, and leaving out punctuation because I'm so excited and in such a hurry to get it all down. I'm not even thinking about what I'm writing.

The enthusiasm has its own energy, and it's an incredible high that we can all tap into. Now, some people are more predisposed to enthusiasm, sure; but it's actually a learned behavior. We can all become more enthusiastic and excited about what we do. If you're enthusiasm-deficient, to coin a term, you need to work on this—because **being more enthusiastic will simply make you more money.** You'll create bigger and better offers, which will cause more people to give you more money, which will cause you to get even more excited, which will cause you to create even bigger offers...

It's a rising spiral, and if you can keep the enthusiasm fueled, it just keeps spiraling higher!

CHAPTER TEN

★★★
You can't have
the glory...
IF YOU DON'T
HAVE THE GUTS!
★★★

You Can't Have the Glory
If You Don't Have the Guts

We've all heard the saying, "No guts, no glory." But it seems like most people just don't get the point—or simply don't want to. So let me clarify: **you can't have the glory,** *if you don't have the guts first.* If you want to make millions of dollars, that money's unlikely to come to you with ease.

It seems like most people just want the benefits of something, without having to put in the time and work necessary to acquire those benefits. They've got no grand plan, they've got no big vision, they have nothing that gets them excited or keeps them excited; and what's even sadder is that **most people don't even *want* glory. All they want is to make a living.** The work they do is just a means to the end of getting a paycheck, so they can feed their family and pay their bills. If they're in business for themselves, it's only to make money. That's all they want; there's no goal beyond that.

You may be thinking, "Well, making money *is* exciting." Sure it is; it's part of the greatest game on Earth. But you can tarnish anything if you do it without enthusiasm; and grinding along just to make some cash is *boring*. When I looked up the word "glory" in the dictionary recently, I found that it means either "honor that is won by notable achievements" or "magnificence." Then I looked up the word "magnificence," and saw that it's just the quality of excellence.

TOTAL SUCCESS!

Most people, even self-employed entrepreneurs, simply want to make a living. **But the greatest entrepreneurs, the ones who are the most successful, the ones whose names go down in history—those people are dedicated and committed to creating things that are bigger, better, new, exciting, bold.** They know how to make money; but they're not interested in just getting by. They want to shine brightly and succeed in the highest possible way. And they do so, because they put it all out there. They know they're not going to cover themselves with glory unless they have the guts to run with the big dogs.

They accomplish what they do by having the guts to try new things—to create something that wasn't there before, something that's audacious, better, and revolutionary. They make their breakthroughs by focusing tightly on their marketplaces, and putting their resources and energy into trying to give their prospects something that no competitor in the market is even close to giving them. They push hard to become the market leader, the entity that the other competitors fear or envy—or at least strive to be more like. They're the leaders of the pack.

The process of moving in that direction, and putting all your focus into creating excellence in your marketplace, is what creates wealth to begin with.

The average employee wants to do just enough to keep his or her job and get that paycheck every couple of weeks. I don't mean this to be a judgment, just an observation. Basically, they're just trying to get through the day, so they have the energy to get through the *next* day. They don't care about doing things in an excellent way. They don't care about trying to

138

be magnificent, or performing at their highest level. They don't really care about the companies they work for, either. They just care about their job, and their place within the company.

Even so, many employees still show up and do a good job. **They're the salt of the earth, and we absolutely, positively need those people.** Every business does. But nonetheless, they're not aiming for excellence. They're not trying to push themselves even harder. They'll do anything you ask them to do, but if you don't ask them to do anything, they won't take the initiative.

The fact is, most people just want to make a living— including most businesspeople. That's the kind of attitude or premise they build their lives on. They've decided they want to move in the direction of making money, and that may in fact be their main focus; and it's ironic that so many people fail at it. The reason is that they're not going for it gung-ho. **They don't have the guts to give it their all... and so the rewards they receive are meager.** The market rewards companies and entrepreneurs for serving it up bigger and better and bolder, for coming up with innovative products and services that cause people to want to do business with them... so why should anyone ever think they should be cautious, staid, or stale?

Well, many of the people who play the game think they're being smart by playing it safe all the time. They think they're being conservative and careful. And granted, they tend not to make the kinds of mistakes that the wild-eyed dreamers make—the reckless, wild, loose-cannon entrepreneurs who are thinking big and bold all the time. Admittedly, those loose cannons also tend to be somewhat wasteful at times, and they do make lots of errors. But all business is calculated risk.

When conservative businessmen decide to play things close to the vest, they often end up overthinking things. Every little move is carefully analyzed and planned out beforehand, because they think that's smart. **Well, what they're really doing is holding back—failing to be innovative to match their changing marketplace.** They continue to sell the same old worn-out stuff, things that don't get people in their market excited... and people just don't want to follow them.

Marketing is all about attracting and retaining customers; and needless to say, in order to attract customers, you have to be attractive. You have to have what people want—especially things they want that they can't get anywhere else. **To accomplish that, you have to be different, which requires a glory-seeking attitude and a willingness to put it all on the line to get there.** You have to fiercely want the magnificent, and to be very proud of what you're doing.

Let's take this back to the Health Resource Portal we're working on here at M.O.R.E., Inc. This is mostly Chris Lakey's baby; I played a small a role in the beginning, but that was about it. We could never have done it without him, because he was the one who had the guts and the know-how to move forward with it. We've cheered him on and backed him all the way, because we know our marketplace is going to go ape over this offer. *Nobody* **has ever done what we're just now starting to do.**

That alone took a lot of guts, because as I've pointed out before, pioneers on any frontier often get scalped. But that's part of what makes the project intriguing and exciting. In fact, I was driving when Chris first told me how unique this project was— and I got so excited I almost drove the car off the road. **The chance to do something so bold and audacious that *nobody* has ever done it before?** I live for that kind of thing! **And to be honest, this is also the kind of thing that causes people to stand in line with money in hand and beg you to take it.** That's what I call "glory" in the business world. I'll take all of that kind of glory I can get.

And yet, most people don't want any glory; they're just trying to make a living. **Even most so-called entrepreneurs are just trying sell whatever's hot; they're not trying to do anything big, bold, and magnificent in any way.** Now, while you *do* have to give the people in your marketplace what they want, the focus on "what's hot now" can stifle your business if you can't take the next step without prompting from the market. Sure, you may take a step in the wrong direction sometimes... but if you're shrewd and careful, you may very well step into a deep pile of money and cover yourself with glory.

Glory never just comes to you; you have to work for it, whether in the boardroom or on the battlefield or the gridiron. **You have to step out and do something that's never been done before; that sums up what this principle is all about.** During the 2011 football season, Chris Lakey told me about how he watched an NFL record fall on a televised game. Sure enough, after the record fell, everyone made a big deal about it. The player who broke the record saluted the crowd, and I'm pretty sure he kept the game football. After the game, SportsCenter was in the locker room, capturing him congratulating the team on celebrating the moment as the coach recognized him. **That's a form of glory that you achieve when something is done in a unique way, or has been done only rarely, or as, in this case, has never been done before.**

If a professional quarterback throws for a few hundred yards in a game, or even throws a touchdown pass, no one really celebrates that unless the touchdown wins them the game. Even then, the celebration is transitory and mild. If a pro baseball player hits 30 homeruns or bats .250 in a baseball season, no one gives him an award for that. Even if a basketball player catches fire and scores 30 or 40 points in a game, no one is likely to celebrate that for long, even though it might have won their team the game. Why? Because people have done it before. It's not a record-breaking performance.

The way to achieve true glory is to have the guts to do what's never been done before... to do things that make people stand up and pay attention. You're sailing in uncharted waters, and it's possible no one else may go there again. For example, there are some sports records on the books that have stood for decades, and may never be broken. It's been done once, and that's it. In the continuum of time, the things that receive the most glory— either for an individual or for a group—are the bigger events. The more likely it is that something won't be repeated, the more the glory associated with it.

Glory isn't to be found in the mundane, the ordinary, the everyday. It's found in the excellent. **You get there by trying to achieve excellence in everything you do.** For example, a professional athlete has to practice hard in order to perform well on the field, and he has to practice a certain way. He can't just slouch off and then expect to perform at peak performance when it counts. So he pushes himself at practice, he does things right, and he takes care of his body all year long—even though the active season is only a few months of the year. That excellence in practice will, hopefully, translate to excellent results on the field.

I urge you to pattern your own behavior after that conscientious professional athlete's. Practice excellence in everything you do, even if it's just preparation or background work. **Try to achieve the best results you possibly can, every time—so you can cover yourself with glory in the marketplace when it counts.** There's an old saying that "practice makes perfect," and that's true enough. But I prefer a correction I once heard in response that goes, "Not necessarily. *Perfect* practice makes perfect."

You have to practice as perfectly as you can. That doesn't mean you'll get it right all the time, but you do have to keep trying until you can do it well; and then you have to keep practicing, so you can achieve perfection (or as near to perfection as a human being can come) in whatever you're trying to do. **The only way to achieve that level of expertise is to do something all the time, over and over—and take a few risks as you reach for the brass ring.** You won't always break records and achieve the glory; things may misfire occasionally, and your risks might not work out.

Let's look at football again. Suppose you're a record-producing quarterback in the NFL. That doesn't mean you perform at that maximum level and get the glory every time you play, even when you've got the guts to put in your maximum effort. It doesn't even mean you win every game. You could own the record, and still throw five interceptions in a game. I mentioned Brett Favre before; he was known for being a Super Bowl-winning quarterback who also threw a *ton* of interceptions, and you kind of accepted that the two went together. He was willing to take the risks necessary to win in a big way, and sometimes those risks didn't pan out, and he failed. **So realize that you can be excellent, and still face undesirable outcomes sometimes.** That doesn't mean you shouldn't reach for that shiny brass ring every time, even when the results don't matter as much and you're really just practicing.

We've faced this reality here at M.O.R.E., Inc. at times. **While we've had million-dollar promotions that achieved optimal success, we've also had things fail spectacularly. When that happens, we go back to the drawing board and try again.** We always seek to achieve excellence and make what we feel are the right decisions, and we'll continue to do so— even when things don't work as we might have liked. Shifting to a baseball metaphor, sometimes we strike out. Then again, sometimes we get a walk, or a single, double, or triple. Every once in a while, we hit a home run; and on rare occasions, we achieve a grand slam or set a record. **Those glorious high points make all the hit-and-miss trials, and all the effort and planning, worthwhile.**

The point is, we're always trying to achieve the best results we can. If you have the guts to give it your all, all the time, and you try to do things that people have never done—if you making going all out all the time a habit—then you *will* eventually achieve the results you're after and break those records. You'll go above and beyond what anyone has ever done before.

You can't get there unless you have the guts to make the regular, constant practice of excellence a part of who you are. If you don't keep trying to hit the mark, you'll never achieve the glory you're looking for... whatever "glory" means to you. It may be fame, the record books, a trophy, cash in the bank, a pat on the back. **Whatever "glory" is, it comes from having the guts to try harder, to go all out, to be the very best you can be.** Conversely, if you just want to be average, do what everybody else is doing. If you just want an average business, do the bare minimum. But beware: in hard times, that may not be enough to keep your business alive.

Putting it all out there, having the guts to practice constant excellence in all aspects of your business, isn't something that most of us are born with. While some of us are naturally more enthusiastic and harder working than others, those are really learned behaviors; they're something you develop. In my book, no one is naturally courageous, either. **Courage is something you have to continue to strive for—and it doesn't mean an absence of fear. Courage is the willingness to keep going in the *face* of fear.** I've often said that if an idea doesn't scare you a little, it's not big enough—and you should just forget it. So courage involves moving on with things that you're afraid of, and ultimately, to looking for bigger and bolder things to do that scare the crap out of you.

You *must* continue to challenge yourself. Do that, and people will naturally be drawn to you—customers, clients, team members, and joint venture partners alike. That's the name of that game.

CHAPTER ELEVEN

People hate to be "sold" — but they love to "choose."

People Hate to Be Sold, But They Love to Choose

Right or wrong, good or bad, we're a materialistic society. We love to buy things; that's part of what makes our economy healthy and strong. Of course, we also have to deal with the planned obsolescence engineered into the products we buy—meaning that they work just fine for a while, and then all of a sudden they fall apart or they become obsolete, and we have to go out and buy replacements. So we're always buying stuff... but the truth is, we love it, planned obsolescence or not. Many times we buy new products even before the old ones wear out, just because we want to have the latest and greatest.

Yet despite the fact that people just love to buy, they hate to be *sold*.

People love to choose things themselves; or at least, to feel that they're the ones making that decision to buy. That means they're the ones who are empowered, not you as the seller. **As soon as people start feeling that you're pressuring them to buy, they'll start running away.** So where does that leave you? You know that the only way you can get rich (whatever that means to you) is to sell enough stuff to enough people, at a large enough profit margin per transaction, as often as possible, with the greatest efficiency. **So how do you overcome this distaste people have for being sold?**

TOTAL SUCCESS!

Simple enough: you let people feel that they're choosing you, even if that's not necessarily the case. There's a true art to this. You have to think deeply about this type of behavior, and you have to observe other people to discover how they're handling it. **Ultimately, it's all about perception.** The more people feel you're chasing after them, or the more they feel pressured, the more they run away from you. But you want people to run *towards* you. **You want people to feel like they're chasing after you.**

The best analogy I have for this is the world of dating. You've heard of the "dance of romance." Sometimes the power struggle, if you will, shifts back and forth a bit; but usually, one of the people in the equation wants it more than the other. This gives the other person some level of power in the relationship. Some people play hard to get so that others are forced to chase them.

Years ago, when I was young and unmarried, I knew this other fellow who was very successful with the ladies. He had no trouble getting one good-looking girlfriend after another. Once, I asked him what his secret was... and he told me it was basically just to let guys like me make fools out of ourselves. He'd let us chase after all the girls, while he sat back and let them come to him. He wasn't playing the same game everybody else was playing. **The fact that he acted like he wasn't interested in chasing girls got a lot of those girls interested in *him*.** He was doing something that other people were not, and it was quite successful for him.

That's a pretty good metaphor for the art of business. People who are good at making money are very much like people who are good at everything else—they make it look effortless. And yet, they had to develop those skills as they went along, and they got better over time. **There are certain skills, methods, and principles involved, and they're learnable by just about anyone.**

Here's a very good principle that you, as a marketer, can use to let people feel as if they're choosing you rather than being sold: two-step marketing. I've talked about it a lot in this book. It's the safest way to make money via marketing, though it can take longer to work than other methods do. In fact, that's the main reason why a lot of marketers *don't* use two-step marketing. But while it does take longer, it's much more effective.

There are many variations of two-step marketing, and sometimes it actually involves multiple steps rather than just two. But in a general sense, even if you're using complicated multi-sequence marketing, there are still two very distinct steps involved. **First, you offer somebody something for low cost or no cost. Second, you make the upsell to something bigger and more profitable.** You stay in touch with them, and continue to do things to try to get them to buy more of whatever it was they bought in the first step. This is where the method can evolve into several or even numerous sub-steps, and become much more complex.

I'll explain some successful two-step marketing we've used here at M.O.R.E., Inc. in a moment, but first I want to point out that you already know a lot about two-step marketing—because other people are using it on you right now. Whenever you see an ad that asks you to call a phone number for more information or send for a free DVD or booklet, or whenever you respond to a low-cost offer and the marketer then tries to sell you something else, they're using two-step marketing on you. **It's a great way to separate out a smaller group of serious people that you know are interested in what you're selling from the general population.** That way, you can spend more money on that smaller group with follow-up marketing, because you're confident that you can make money with them with your upsell.

What makes this effective is that in the end, your customers feel as if they're the ones who came to you... and they did, by responding to your offer. If that sounds a little illogical, remember that purchasing is often based on emotion rather logic. The group of prospects that you've qualified with the first step of your marketing plan tend to forget they responded to you in the first place. **They feel that they're the ones that sought you out.** And again, in a way, that's true: they're the ones who called that phone number, sent for the free DVD, or paid $29.95 for a low-cost offer. They usually fail to consider that they were responding to your call, though, so they feel that they, as the chasers, have control of the relationship. They feel empowered; and as a result, they don't feel you're selling to them. Instead, they feel they're seeking you out to buy—which, again, people love to do.

To reiterate, the secret to getting rich is to sell more stuff to more people, more often, for more profit, with greater efficiency. You can put that secret on a 3x5 card and keep it with you. Think deeply about it; really analyze it. **Once you have, it all comes down to how you leverage that secret—i.e., what you implement to actually get people to buy from you.** This can become a very complicated process, so much so that it can take years to figure out the best methods to do it. But at its root, it's still simple two-step marketing; so whenever you get confused, just go back to the basics. And remember that two-step marketing generates many billions of dollars every year, so it obviously works very well indeed.

Here's an example of how we've use two-step marketing to make millions of dollars at M.O.R.E., Inc. **We have a website promotion we call our "Beta Tester Offer." We've tried many different variants over the years, but our current versions ultimately sell a $3,995 package.** Now, in a perfect world we'd just go out there with one step. We'd say, "Hey, here's our offer, and it costs $3,995. Here are all the things we're promising to give you in exchange for you giving us that money." People would read the offer, take a good hard look at all that they were getting for the price, and then reach for their credit cards. It would be a very fast, effective process. **But here in the real world, an offer like that would make people feel like they were under too much pressure. That would make them run away.**

Therefore, the first package we offer is phenomenally low-priced. It gives the customer so much value for such a small amount of money that it just blows them away. **If they're really good prospective buyers, people who will ultimately give us $3,995 for the full package, the offer is irresistible: so powerful they simply cannot refuse it.** To determine what works best for hooking these folks, we test different prices. On this one project, we're actually testing a $9 offer and a $99 offer that essentially provide the same thing. **The difference here is that we know that people who spend $99 are much more**

serious than those who spend $9.

In either case, the idea is to blow them away with the value and quality of this small chip off the bigger block of our $4,000 offer — to impress them so fully they're more likely to step up to the larger package. Once we've gotten their attention and they know they can trust us, they're ready for the next step. Think of that first offer as like going out for a cup of coffee in the dating world, or maybe having a slice of pie at Denny's. You're just getting to know each other... and it's a single small step, no big deal. But if you can impress the other person, and they like you, that sets you up for a more elaborate date, which in business involves pitching more of what they bought from you on that first step. It may take a series of these "dates" to work your way up to the big sell.

So think of the first step as a miniature version of the larger step you want them to take in the end. It makes the upsell seamless when you do it properly, because it not only qualifies your prospect (so you know they're interested in what you have), it lets them feel that they came to you. **Since they chose you, when you make that upsell offer, they don't feel pressured at all.** In fact, they feel empowered; so they end up buying more from you, and that's how you make your real profit.

In my opinion, two-step marketing is simply one of the best methods of reaching people in a way that doesn't make them feel they're being sold. In a true free market, people respond for any reason, or no reason at all… but ultimately, the buying and selling of goods happens as people make their own choices regarding what they want to buy and how they're going to buy it. We don't have a completely free marketplace, of course; government regulation, taxation, and other coercion have their effects. Sometimes a government props up a certain segment of the marketplace for reasons of its own, good or bad. One example today is the "green" marketplace, where in an effort to save the environment the government has done things like subsidize the electric car industry. At this point, it's a miniscule marketplace that would collapse under normal market forces, since most people don't want to buy electric cars. But the government offers a tax rebate and tax credits not only to the manufacturers of those vehicles, but also to the buyers, and so people take advantage of that—and the market survives.

They're doing the same thing by pushing people toward using compact fluorescent and LED light bulbs instead of old-fashioned incandescent bulbs, via government regulation and pricing. That's the opposite of free market, really. But absent tax incentives, credits, and other government manipulation, people do make their own decisions regarding how they're going to spend their money; and there are all kinds of factors that influence that. While you can and should study the marketplace closely, there's no way to account for every factor—and you can't always guess what the market will be interested in, which is why some new ideas fail in the marketplace, while others thrive. You can't *will* your product to be liked by the marketplace. **You do your research, you hope that you've found a product your marketplace likes, you put it out there and wait for the results… and hopefully they're positive.** Remember, people hate to be sold, but they love to choose. **That's what a free economy is all really about: people choosing what they'll buy.**

TOTAL SUCCESS!

A common decision people have to make is, "Where will I eat tonight?" One option is to go to the market, pick up some food, then prepare a meal in your own kitchen. If you don't like that option, you can go to McDonald's. If you don't like McDonald's or fast food in general, you can find a place that serves sit-down meals, and maybe have a salad, or a steak, or both. You can choose to go wherever you want for dinner. This is how the free market works.

Similarly, if you need some construction work done, you can figure out how to do it yourself with the tools you have, go to a hardware store and buy the right tools and supplies, or just hire someone to do everything for you. It's up to you, with certain broad constraints, to choose the course of action you're going to take to achieve the results you're looking for. If someone's interested in losing weight, they'll have to choose from a dieting method and various supplements. If they're into nutrition, they might shop the health market for a good vitamin. If they're looking for an automobile, they'll have to peruse the car lots searching for one that matches their criteria, or just catches their imagination the right way. **In all these cases, the consumer is choosing to purchase based on their own desires, goals, wants, and dreams.**

All that happens in a free market economy. Not to be too political here, but I'm not sure we've had a true free market economy for many years—but we do have some semblance of it. We all have many, many choices about what we can do with our money; and we make such choices every day, throughout our adult lives. **Mostly, we actually *like* buying things—though, again, we *hate* being sold.** Think about it: it's during some of the most obvious times that we're being sold that we rebel against salesmanship the most. Have you ever received a telemarketing phone call while eating dinner? Don't you hate when that happens? They flat-out tell you they're trying to sell you something, and it's clear they don't respect your free time, so the ensuing discussion often isn't a pleasant one. Usually you try to get off the phone as fast as possible. And if you're like millions of other Americans, your name is already on the "DO NOT CALL" list because you don't like to be sold.

The same is true if the doorbell rings during dinner, and it's someone who has come to try to get you to buy a service or sell you some magazines or cookies. **Usually, if you even open your door, you're not happy that you did—because you end up talking to a salesman without it being on *your* terms.** That's why some people have "No Soliciting" signs on their doors. They just don't like to be sold.

But the truth is, in a massive economy like ours, where millions of transactions occur on a daily basis despite the built-in resistance to selling... well, obviously nothing gets bought unless it's sold in some way. Even when I go to Wal-Mart to voluntarily purchase something, at some level that product has been sold to me.

So how do you get people from feeling like they're being sold to choosing to buy? **Well, that's one reason we're so in favor of two-step marketing, because you basically use this methodology to get people to request your sales material.** In their eyes, they're choosing to buy; and once you've got the door open, you can sell harder to them, because they've proven they're interested in buying. Now, two-step marketing can be done in any number of ways. We happen to be direct response marketers. Most of our business is done by mail or on the Internet, but the basic methodology can apply to print publications, billboards, TV ads, etc; you could even do it over the phone or with a local retail store. The concept is the same no matter what its format and final appearance. **Specifically, you get people to request information from you or do something to indicate an interest in what you have to sell.** Then you can approach them as someone who was invited, instead of as someone trying to get something from them.

If you're in the marketplace for carpet cleaning because it's been a long, messy winter and your carpets are dirty, and you don't want to buy or rent a cleaner yourself (another option in the free market), then you'll need someone to do the job for you. So you open the Yellow Pages or you look online and find out who offers that service in your area; and maybe you see an ad that looks interesting to you. Then you make a phone call, or go on the website for more information. **Ultimately, you show the providers you're interested in the service, and maybe you invite one or two to come into your home and give you a bid.** Because you sought out carpet cleaners in the first place, you receive those bids much more positively than you would have if they'd just showed up on your doorstep and made a pitch. That happens in all kinds of businesses, in all kinds of ways.

Since we mostly sell by mail, when we do a two-step marketing offer, our prospect first receives a small envelope or package. If they decide it's not worth their time, or it's not something that interests them at the moment, they can toss it and they'll never hear from us again (at least regarding that offer).

We don't pay much attention to people who say no, because obviously they're not the people we're after.

What we're looking for is the people who look at our offer and say, "That's something I'm interested in. I'm going to raise my hand, put myself on the line, and request information about this. I'm going to invite this company into my home via mail to tell me more about this offer." **From that moment forward, we're an invited guest. They've given us permission to provide more information about what we're selling... and we *will* do that.** During our follow-up, we'll send them a package or call them on the phone to answer any questions they have, because they've literally asked us to do so.

We've arranged that politely. We didn't go barging into their home unannounced (either physically or by phone) and try to get them interested in an offer. That's the difference between something being sold, and somebody choosing to make a purchase. **You carefully arrange to give your prospects the opportunity to be consumers, which they want to be anyway, and let them decide where to spend their money.** You're just encouraging them to spend it with you.

Don't forget that if they don't spend it with you, they're going to spend their discretionary cash somewhere. There are exceptions to every rule, but almost all of us love to be consumers. We love to spend money on things that we think will make us feel better, look better, smell better, live better—or whatever the case may be. We're all looking for improvement in the areas of our lives that are important to us.

Collectively, we Americans spend billions of dollars yearly

to accomplish that, despite the fact that we honestly do everything possible to avoid being sold things. We'll practically run the other direction to avoid it... and sometimes we literally do. It's happened in my own household. Ever head for the basement when someone rings the doorbell? Sometime when the phone rings, you just don't answer it, because it may be a telemarketer—right?

As a marketer, the way you break through obstacles like that is by getting people to choose to do business with you. **This is the basis of all two-step marketing.** There are other things you can do to convince people to buy, but this way is best. **The more you can make people feel like they're asking for the privilege of doing business with you, the more you'll win in this marketplace.** Whatever you sell, get people to feel like *they're* in control, not you. "Run until they catch you," as they say in the dating world.

When you play hard to get, the power shifts to your side of the equation... even though the other person is likely to feel that they're in control, because they've taken the initiative. Most people like to feel that they're making the active choice. They like to chase—but they don't necessarily like to *be* chased, and be subjected to high pressure.

In this world, we're all trying to protect ourselves. **Each of us wants to be the one to choose; we don't want other people to choose for us.**

CHAPTER TWELVE

Spend <u>more</u> money — to close more sales!

1. You can't go wrong if you are spending this money on super qualified prospects.

2. You are selling big ticket items with good margins.

In some cases (as long as your percentage of conversion is going up) you can't spend too much money!

Spend More Money to Close More Sales

Too many marketers try to close sales as cheaply as they can, and that's a big mistake: you should do the exact opposite, and spend *more* money to close those sales. Ultimately, this tactic is vastly more profitable, assuming you're spending the money on super-qualified prospects—especially if you're selling big-ticket items with high profit margins. **In fact, as long as your conversion percentage is high and you've got a big pool of well-qualified prospective buyers, it's hard to go wrong— you almost can't spend too much money, because well-qualified prospective buyers are insatiable.** They simply can't get enough of what you're selling.

P. T. Barnum, the great showman, has widely been quoted as saying, "There's a sucker born every minute." He never really said that, but one thing he did say was, "Most people are trying to catch a whale by using a minnow as bait." In other words, most marketers want to make the largest amount of money possible by spending as little money as they can. **On the face of it, that *sounds* like a good idea, since you're cutting expenses; but at the end of the day, it's a huge mistake, because the big fish aren't interested in tiny baits.** They want something meaty, something big enough to taste.

You really do have to spend money to make money. As long as you're dealing with a good, qualified prospective buyer—somebody who's likely to end up spending a lot of money with you over a long period of time, somebody who really, really wants the kind of products and services you have to offer—then if you build big enough profit margin into your offers, you almost can't spend too much money when trying to convert prospects to sales.

Let's take another look at two-step marketing, which is probably the most proven way of getting rich in the marketing world. Not only are you letting people feel that they're choosing you rather than you choosing them, you're letting people qualify themselves by the specific action you're asking them to take with your low cost or no-cost front end—e.g., that first offer. **By their actions, the prospects are proving to you that they're qualified, and serious about what you're selling.**

Like my Grandma Clara used to say, "The only way you can tell anything about a person is by the actions they take." **You can also tell a lot about people by the actions they *don't* take.** If you mail your front-end offer to a group of people and most don't take that initial step, then they're proving to you they're not going to take the second step, either. **So you don't waste money on them; you pour it into the smaller group of people who respond to your initial offer.** They've proved to you they're serious and qualified.

Your follow-up sequence might include phone calls, teleseminars, other low-ticket items to pique their interest, or direct mail. If you have a local business, you can sponsor or create local events. You might even send one of your salespeople over to answer the prospect's questions. **No matter how you do it, if someone has proved they're a qualified prospect, then**

you've got to stay after them—and keep staying after them. Remember: just because somebody says "no" or doesn't respond after they initially qualify themselves, that doesn't mean they're always going to say no. **If you've qualified them properly, you just have to hang in there and continue to follow-up.**

Shortly after we first got started in the business, I worked with a famous marketer to put together a 30-minute infomercial that we ran in 14 different test cities. It was a two-step offer and, sure enough, people responded in droves. **We followed up somewhat, but we just couldn't get our conversion rates high enough to make a profit;** in fact, we weren't making enough sales to cover the cost of that infomercial. Well, this famous marketer kept telling me over and over, "You're giving up on them too soon," because I was very upset that we weren't making money. The more I argued with him, the more he just kept saying that. I was very frustrated and angry because we were trying all kinds of things to follow up, to no avail; and it sounded to me like he was just shining me on with some generality.

Well, I've thought about that a lot since... and decided that we really *were* giving up too soon. We weren't keeping the pressure on the prospects, we weren't following up enough, and we weren't being disruptive enough in their lives. **They had responded to our initial offer, so we should have been following up with them a whole lot more.**

I've learned my lesson since then. **Nowadays, we're relentless follow-up marketers.** Once somebody responds to one of our front-end offers, we keep the pressure on. They've invited us in and we believe strongly in what we're selling, so we're not taking advantage of anybody by doing this. We know that our products and services produce the results that our clients are looking for. And as long as that's true, **as long as you know that what you have to offer really *does* help people get more of whatever it is they want, and as long as you know that those people really are qualified for your offers, then you're doing them a disservice if you don't do everything possible (short of physical violence) to sell it to them.**

To accomplish this, you have to spend money, and you have to do things that separate you from everybody else. Never forget how distracted people are, and how busy they are. Just because somebody who initially responded hasn't responded to your latest follow-up doesn't mean they never will. You know they're serious, or they wouldn't have raised their hand on the front end; so keep pushing. **Even if they don't respond the first ten times, they might respond on the eleventh.** We've had some sequences that have gone as high as 20-30 pieces on the follow-up. We just keep following up, following up, and following up. We keep coming at them different ways. We keep that pressure on. That's what salespeople do. All the best salespeople will stay after a prospect. They'll keep banging on that door until somebody opens it.

It all starts with doing everything you can to get people to qualify themselves, to prove to you that they really are serious by the actions they take. **Then you follow-up like crazy, spend more money on the smaller group of people that have qualified themselves.** If you've done everything possible and people still don't convert, then the first step you ask them to take has to be increased, so they'll *really* prove they're serious. You have to try to get them to do more on that first step—to spend even more money, or take more of an action. We've had some deals where we've asked people to listen to a one-hour recording that was going to sell them something for a couple of thousand dollars. Why? Because anyone willing to listen to the full recording *must* to be serious. **Once they've proven that, we stay on top of them. You've got to, in order to make that sale.**

Now, realize that even if people have qualified themselves, if they feel like they're under too much pressure, they're going to run away. So you have to lay your plans carefully, well in advance, and **be subtle with the pressure. Come at people in as altruistic a way as possible. It has to be all about them and what you're offering to do for them; the results, the benefits, the value they're going to get. Never let it be about you.** Show them what you can give to them, and how much you want to help them, and how much you want to serve them, and how much value they'll receive, and how their lives will change when they buy your product. **Often, you have to get creative about how you approach your prospects; and your methodology has to be a little different every time.** But you're still applying that subtle pressure. Keep spending the money you need to, and spend it wisely, to convert more sales and make more profits.

The key word here is "wisely." Sometimes marketers can get stuck in this mindset that you have to spend more money to make more money... and they forget about the need to get people to qualify themselves. Worse, they forget about the metrics underlying their marketing efforts. There are scores of ways you could spend your advertising dollars; but **if you're not doing something to measure that advertising's**

effectiveness, how do you know whether or not it worked?
How can you know, at the end of the day, what you should
spend more money on, and what you should stop doing,
because it's not cost-effective? Of course, **if you're only
spending money on one marketing method, it's easy to
gauge your success.** But if you're doing multiple things at
once, or testing subtly different things to see what works best,
you absolutely have to keep a sharp eye on the metrics.

It's not *just* about spending more money. **It's about being
smart about spending more money, and closing more sales as
a result.**

Again, this is why we love two-step marketing here at
M.O.R.E., Inc. **People qualify themselves on the front end,
thinning the herd if you will, so we can focus our efforts on
a few people at a time.** That lets us spend more money while
we're chasing those sales, trying to close as many as possible.
Just to use a round number, let's say you had 1,000 people that
you wanted to send a new offer to. Well, it would cost you a
huge amount of money to go out to those 1,000 people and
make a full, effective sales presentation to each of them,
striving to sell your big product in one step. Unfortunately, you
might be wasting your time with a lot of them, because for
some reason or other they didn't want or need your product or
service at the moment.

But suppose that instead of automatically making that full
sales effort to every single person, you just sent them a small
"teaser" or lead generation offer that let them decide whether
they wanted to hear your presentation. **And let's say only 10%
raised their hands. That's a drastic reduction, but now you**

know for certain that each person in that smaller group is interested in hearing from you. In fact, they've asked you to make your presentation... so they're chasing you now. Remember, people hate to be sold, but they love to choose.

So at this point, instead of 1,000 people feeling sold, you've got 100 people who've chosen to request information from you. You can make your full presentation to them, whether that involves sending them a direct mail package or having a salesman call them or even show up on their doorstep. **While you may not make 100 sales, at least you've cleared out most of the people who are never going to buy anything from you, so you can serve the people who might more fully.** You can afford to spend more money on each of them... money you might have wasted on those other 900 people who really weren't interested. In all likelihood, you'll close more sales out of those 100 prospects who requested information from you than you'd close on the group of 1,000 who hadn't heard anything about your offer before... and you'll obtain those customers at a lower overall cost. **You can afford to spend more money converting those people into paying customers simply because they belong to a group that's more responsive to your offer.**

That's what this strategy is all about. You can't go wrong if you're spending this money on super-qualified prospects, people who have willingly jumped through a few hoops already. And again, this assumes you're selling big-ticket items with good profit margins. **If you're selling something inexpensively, there's probably not enough money in it to spend a lot of money on advertising;** so you have to be careful here, too, when you're using this strategy. Again, you must apply it wisely.

TOTAL SUCCESS!

Let's say that you're selling a top-notch product or service for several thousand dollars. How many of your 100 self-qualified prospects are likely to buy what you're selling? Let's say 20% (2% of the original thousand) end up buying. **If each purchased a $5,000 package, you just made $100,000 net.** That's an excellent income from 20 customers—so you can afford to spend a lot to covert them.

You could do things like FedExing them a special invitation—or send them $20 bills to make a good impression. We've actually done that before. I've heard of people sending out one fancy dress shoe, with an invitation to get together so the prospect could get the other. This was a face-to-face selling technique, of course, but with a little imagination, you might adapt it to other methods. In this case, I suppose you'd have to go all covert ops and talk to a secretary at their office to find out the shoe size of the person you were trying to reach. The point is, if you were trying to make a sales presentation to an executive of some Fortune 500 Company, sending them a nice, fancy shoe might get their attention, and make them pick up the phone and call you.

There are all kinds of things you can do to attract their attention. Needless to say, it's not hard to spend money; **but you have to make sure you're spending it on the right people.** That's why sending a full offer to a thousand people is unlikely to be as profitable as getting a hundred prospects that raise their hand. **When you do that, when you can focus the persuasive power of your budget on just a few people, you're much better off.** A sharp edge, applied surgically, is much more effective than a dull one that you just hack away with in any direction.

Don't try to be cheap here; buck the natural tendency to spend as little as possible on your qualified prospects. **The biggest part of your budget should be spent converting those leads to sales.** So use the two-step marketing method to first attract the smaller group of people who are interested in what you have to sell, and then spend your money and resources doing all you can to get that smaller group of prospects to become customers. Since there are all kinds of ways that you could do this, you'll need to experiment with different methods, and find out what works best for you.

If your margins are right, the numbers will all work out, and you'll end up still making a very healthy profit—which gives you more money to plug back into attracting more of that kind of customer the second and third and fourth times around. Just keep the system moving. In two-step marketing, you're always running out there with your lead generation offers to attract new customers, getting them to request information, and then converting the biggest percentage of those prospects possible into paying customers. **Beyond that, your profit comes from doing more business with your existing customers.** When done right, the system can produce very healthy profits for your company—and it can basically run on autopilot, as long as you keep the machine well oiled.

If it sounds simple, that's because it *is* simple. It's not necessarily easy, but the process is simple; and it's good to know that it is. Whenever you get confused, just go back to that. I'll admit that it can be a lot of work; but it can also be a lot of fun. That's what you should focus on. **Don't listen to your fears, or**

let all the obstacles worry you. Focus on the outcome, and make a game out of it. Keep score with money... and realize that the profit potential is high, easily in the hundreds of thousands or millions of dollars. That's always exciting!

In your mind, emphasize the thrill of the hunt. Don't start thinking, "Oh my goodness, what if this goes wrong? What if this screws up?" That's the wrong mentality; you should be *eager* to meet the challenge. You should be excited about it. **When somebody responds to one of your initial offers, they're proving to you that they're serious, so you should go after them aggressively.** Again, you're trying to make it all about altruism—about giving and serving and helping. **If you really have something that can change people's lives, you should pursue the sale with a missionary zeal.** Approach it from the standpoint that you're helping them. You're serving them, not trying to take anything away from them, or trying to get them to do anything.

See it as a game. It's creative; it's challenging. Again, in a way it's like fishing. You're trying to reel in the biggest fish you can; so you have to provide it with a bait it will notice and be attracted to. Look at it as an adventure. **If you're not sure what to do, then study how successful people are accomplishing what you want to accomplish, so you can model yourself after them.** Find the best players in your market, get on their mailing lists, and spend some money with those people. In fact, be willing to spend quite a bit of money. Look at how they're following up with you—and just emulate them. You don't have to be a genius to make money this way; I myself am very successful at it, and I'll be the first to admit I'm not the sharpest pencil in the box. **But I *am* determined and stubborn, and I'm willing to learn.** I see successful people who aren't as smart as I am, and they do fine because they know how to follow the leader.

Frankly, that's a good way to start. Then, after a while, you learn how to be a little innovative and throw some of your own ideas into the mix, and it becomes more than just making money. **It becomes a whole lifestyle, something you can put your heart, soul, and passion into.** It becomes deeply fulfilling—very, very satisfying, like a hobby that you can lose yourself in for hours at a time. That's the kind of thing that I'm talking about here. So whenever you start thinking the opposite, stop, consider what you're doing, get your head together—and get back in the game!